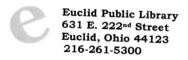

GAME OF MY LIFE

CLEVELAND

BROWNS

MEMORABLE STORIES OF BROWNS FOOTBALL

MATT LOEDE

SPORTS
PUBLISHING

Sports Publishing books may be purchased in bulk at special discounts for sales promotion, corporate gifts, fund-raising, or educational purposes. Special editions can also be created to specifications. For details, contact the Special Sales Department, Sports Publishing, 307 West 36th Street, 11th Floor, New York, NY 10018 or sportspubbooks@skyhorsepublishing.com.

Sports Publishing® is a registered trademark of Skyhorse Publishing, Inc.®, a Delaware corporation.

Visit our website at www.sportspubbooks.com.

10 9 8 7 6 5 4 3 2 1

Library of Congress Cataloging-in-Publication Data is available on file.

Cover design by Tom Lau
Cover photo credit Associated Press

ISBN: 978-1-61321-939-3
Ebook ISBN: 978-1-61321-944-7

Printed in the United States of America

CONTENTS

INTRODUCTION

FOR THE CITY of Cleveland and the fans of the Browns, it's not just a football team; for many, it's a way of life. From rabid fan clubs all around the country to fans around Northeast Ohio wearing the colors of the brown and orange, time stops when the Browns take the field each week.

Founded in 1945 by a local businessman, Arthur McBride, and coached by the legendary Hall of Fame coach Paul Brown, it didn't take long for the Browns to be a success. They joined the NFL in 1949 and won a championship their first year in the league, then went on to win three more, the last of which was in 1964 when they shut out the Baltimore Colts, 27–0, at Cleveland Municipal Stadium.

Since then fans have been waiting, through the good years and the bad, for glory to return to the Browns franchise. They have had to endure the harshest of defeats, losing three times to the Denver Broncos in the 1980s, on the doorstep of playing in their first Super Bowl.

They also had to live out the nightmare of their franchise being ripped away during the 1995 season, as then owner Art Modell moved them to Baltimore in one of the most shocking moves in NFL history.

Fans stood by their team, and three years later in the midst of fanfare there was a rebirth in 1999, as a new owner, a new stadium, and a new team took the colors of old and returned to the lakefront. This book will give you an idea of the fanfare and the love that former players and fans have for the Cleveland Browns.

Read as former players talk of the glory days, of NFL titles, and of exciting trips to the postseason. You'll understand after reading this just how much Cleveland loves its football team, and how the players feel the same.

The 22 players spoken to for this book have an array of great stories and great memories. From some of the more painful games in the history of the franchise, to exciting wins that defined some of the club's great players, this team and the players we spoke to shared with us some of their best memories of Browns football.

I hope you enjoy it as much as I enjoyed talking to the players and writing it.

CHAPTER 1

DOUG DIEKEN

Offensive Tackle 1971–1984
The Game: December 21, 1980, vs Cincinnati Bengals at
Riverfront Stadium
CLEVELAND BROWNS 27—CINCINNATI BENGALS 24

WHEN YOU THINK that you've sat and watched a ton of Cleveland Browns football games over the course of your life, there's one person who almost certainly can beat you at that number.

Not only that, he's done it live.

That person is former Browns offensive tackle and current radio color commentator Doug Dieken, who has been with the Browns organization in two different capacities for over four decades.

"I guess I could say I've probably seen more Browns games live than any person that's ever lived," Dieken said. "I think we're up in the 800s if you count the preseason games."

Dieken as a player remains one of the best in the history of the franchise, and his voice will go down as one that many Browns fans grew up with, and still hear on game days.

Born in Streator, Illinois, in February of 1949, Dieken played his high school ball at Streator High before going to college at nearby Illinois, where he would become the second-leading receiver in Fighting Illini history.

At the school he played both wide receiver and tight end, and in his college career hauled in 89 passes for 1,246 yards and seven touchdowns.

Notes on Doug Dieken

Years Played: 1971-1984
Position: Offensive tackle
Height: 6'5"
Weight: 254
Hometown: Streator, IL
Current Residence: Westlake, OH
Occupation: Color commentator for the Cleveland Browns Radio Network, Sports Time Ohio Analyst
Accomplishments: Played high school ball in Streator, IL, before going to Illinois for college. He played tight end and wide out in college, and in his time there caught 89 passes for 1,246 yards and seven touchdowns. Was a sixth-round pick of the Browns in 1974. Started five games his rookie season and then for the next ten seasons played in each and every game before playing in nine games in 1982. Caught a touchdown on a fake field goal from Paul McDonald in a game on November 30, 1983, against the Oilers in a 23–17 win, his only NFL catch. Was named the Byron "Whizzer" White NFL Man of the Year in 1982 and was the Browns' team offensive MVP in 1975. Was a Pro Bowl offensive tackle in 1980. Holds the franchise records for consecutive games played (203) and consecutive starts (193). Moved to the broadcast booth in 1984 and has been the team's color commentator since 1985.
Nickname: None

Henry Sheppard and Doug Dieken (r) share a laugh. (Cleveland Press Collection)

He was hopeful that his career catching passes would continue in the NFL. Instead, the Browns had other plans when they took him in the sixth round of the 1971 NFL Draft.

"When I got the call from Nick Skorich, he told me that they drafted me in the sixth round as a tackle," Dieken recalls. "I asked him, 'Is there any chance I can play tight end?' and he said, 'We'll see when you get here.'

"Well, when I got to rookie camp they gave me the number 73, so I said to myself this doesn't look good in terms of my tight end career."

Making the switch full-time to offensive tackle was no easy task, and Dieken didn't have a ton of time to try and make the switch, position-wise, before he was thrown into the fire by the Browns.

By the middle of his rookie season in 1971, he was getting playing time on the line and by the end of his first season started five games.

"As a rookie, you didn't play much, so I probably played about three quarters of my rookie year in games for the first time in my life as a tackle," Dieken said.

"Probably about six games into my rookie year the right tackle got hurt, so they put me in at right tackle, and I had been playing at left tackle behind Dick Schafrath, and I was able to survive, and a couple weeks later I became the starting left tackle.

"So I became a starter in the NFL with about five quarters of experience playing; it was kind of jungle warfare in terms of how you played. You played to survive, not to lose, and if you tended to lose you turned it into a street fight, and I was able to do it for 14 years."

Not only was Dieken a starter for the remainder of his career, he still holds the franchise records for consecutive games played (203) and consecutive starts (193).

The Browns as a team, though, were getting ready to go through a hard stretch. They won their last NFL Championship in 1964 but were still a very good football team, challenging for another title for a number of years after that.

They finished first in the Century Division of the Eastern Conference in 1967, '68, and '69, and in their first season in the AFC Central in 1970, they finished second in the division.

In 1971, Dieken's first season, and 1972, the Browns made the postseason but lost their first playoff game in each of the two seasons.

"I got to the Browns, and the first two years we were in the playoffs," Dieken recalls. "We had a lot of guys on the old '64 championship team still on the roster, and you expected on Sunday with those guys that you were going to win.

"Well, then, these guys all started to retire about the same age and we didn't do the best job drafting, and the next thing you know we had some tough years and started to go through coaches."

From 1973 to 1979, the team had three winning seasons, then struggled to reach the heights they had enjoyed during the 1950s to late 1960s, when they were winning NFL Championships.

Things finally started to turn around in 1979 when, under coach Sam Rutigliano, the team went 9–7, and it seemed like things were finally starting to turn the corner.

Then came 1980, the the year that Browns fans to this day still remember as the season of the "Kardiac Kids."

"It was kind of a special time to play football in Cleveland," Dieken points out. "Having gone to the playoffs in '71 and '72, and even having a season starting out 0–9, it was appreciative."

The 1980 season was full of fun for the brown and orange. From wild finishes that saw the Browns pull out miracle wins, to MVP Brian Sipe having a career-year, it was a fun time to root for the Browns.

"Sometimes we won in pretty style, sometimes it was ugly," Dieken remembers. "There was a game that year against the Green Bay Packers where Dave Logan caught a touchdown pass at the end of the game to win it for us.

"I also remember getting three holding penalties in the game and thinking, 'If we don't win this, I'm going to be the shmuck.'"

The team was 10–4 before they lost a tough game in Minnesota, 28–23, in week 15. It set up a final week of the regular season matchup with the Cincinnati Bengals, a game that would determine if the Browns would live to fight another day.

The Game

In 1980 we got back into the playoffs, and the signature game of that season was late in the year when we went down to Cincinnati, and we had to win or we'd be out of the playoffs.

We were able to win that game, but by the same token our offensive line had the lead for the least amount of sacks per pass attempt, and in that game we gave up six sacks.

We probably didn't play up to what we hoped to in terms of keeping the sacks down, but we did get to return to the playoffs, which of course led to the "Red Right 88" game.

It was one of those "win or go home" games, and it enabled us to get into the playoffs. I do remember we won the game, and I do remember after the game we had some sort of airplane malfunction.

Of course, if you win in Cincinnati the showers in the locker room are never warm; they're ice cold.

A couple games before, we played down in Houston against the Oilers and won, and came back and at the airport there was just so many people there. That was the era where you still flew through the gate.

The place was just jammed with people, so then after the Cincinnati game they had us land outside the IX Center, and there was a bunch of people there, the Mayor of Cleveland, George Voinovich.

I'm introducing him to all the guys, but obviously when we were stuck in Cincinnati we found the airport restaurant and bar, so we were feeling no pain.

So I'm introducing the mayor around to different people and the players, and next thing I know he was late getting up on the platform to introduce the team.

Back to the game, the way that game went is we had everything to lose and the Bengals had nothing to play for. We got down, 10–0, and we caught a bomb and that really got us going.

That seemed to get the wheels in gear and things got going after that; we got the win, and we got our cold shower and got to the airplane.

Brian Sipe was our quarterback; that was the season he won the NFL MVP award. He came my second year, and he was just a guy, but he was just a winner in so many ways.

He was a catcher on a Little League team that won the Little League World Series, but he wasn't the prototypical NFL quarterback.

He wasn't 6-foot-4 and didn't have the cannon arm. What Brian had was, he had a lot of poise as well as the understanding of the game; he made up for what he lacked in arm strength with anticipation.

That 1980 year was special in a lot of ways; we just had great team chemistry.

Everything around the city was "Kardiac Kids"; to this day people still come up and say to me that was their favorite era of Browns football with all the close games we won.

The Aftermath

The celebration of the win over the Bengals was short-lived, as two weeks later, on January 4, 1981, the team played the infamous game at Cleveland Stadium known to all for the famous call of "Red Right 88."

The playoff loss to the Raiders ended the exciting 1980 season, one that is talked about to this day as one of the most memorable in Browns history.

"It was a disappointment, and I remember my brother and other people who were in town for it," Dieken said. "After the game we went out to eat; I wanted to go home and he coaxed me into going out.

"We went to this place, Victoria Station, that was our place back in that era, and all the sadness of not being able to continue the season, the people that you ran into that night, they were disappointed, too, but the first thing they came up and said was, 'Thanks for a great season.'

"It wasn't what you had hoped for, but it was nice people appreciated your efforts for that season."

The loss to the Raiders started another tough stretch over the next few seasons for the Browns, as they wouldn't make another playoff appearance until the 1985 season, a year after Dieken retired after 14 seasons.

It certainly wasn't the end of Dieken with the Browns organization, though, as the former lineman joined the Browns radio crew and eventually became the color commentator for all of the team's games, something he's now done for nearly 30 years.

"Obviously, as a broadcaster, it's a lot more fun when they win over when they lose; you feel for the guys and don't want to be too critical," Dieken said.

He's still one of the most recognizable players in the history of the team, regarded as one of the best linemen in team history after playing in 193 straight games, still to this day a Browns record.

Dieken is also very active in charity. He is the founder of the Doug Dieken Foundation, a nonprofit that helps underwrite the Special Olympics.

He was honored in 1982 as the Byron "Whizzer" White NFL Man of the Year and in 2012 received the Lifetime Achievement Award at the Greater Cleveland Sports Awards.

His career is littered with awards and honors; he was the team captain for a number of seasons and also won team offensive MVP honors in 1975. He was a Pro Bowler in 1980, as well.

To this day he enjoys what he does, being part of the radio team and spending time in Berea at the Browns' training complex and headquarters.

He also still has a special relationship with the fans, from those who rooted for him as a player to those who now listen to him every week on the team's broadcasts.

"The difference between then and now, the players they have the valet parking in the stadium, when in the old days you parked your car across the street in the parking lot, so after the game you walked out of the stadium, you didn't have to know what the score was, by the time you got to the car you knew if it was a good game or a bad game," Dieken said.

"There was a bit of accountability for the players, you couldn't hide, you were exposed and constructive criticism was good; it wasn't always constructive, but that's the way the town was.

"It was a great relationship with the players and the fans."

Dieken still shares in that relationship, but in a different way: from the broadcast booth instead of the playing field. But the bond between him and the Browns is stronger than ever.

CHAPTER 2

ANDRA DAVIS

Linebacker 2002–2008

The Game: September 7, 2003, vs Indianapolis Colts at Browns Stadium

INDIANAPOLIS COLTS 9—CLEVELAND BROWNS 6

ANDRA DAVIS WAS a player the Cleveland Browns organization was fortunate to have, a player who played with everything he had during his seven years with the organization.

Davis was drafted by the Browns in the fifth round out of Florida in 2002, taken with the 141st pick. He was recognized as a first-team All-SEC selection, and a second-team All-American in his senior season in Florida.

The Browns watched him closely leading up to draft day and pulled the trigger on the linebacker in the fifth round.

"Them drafting me out of college and taking a chance on me, my time in Cleveland was absolutely amazing," Davis recalls.

"When I was drafted I didn't know very much about the team, but being able to learn and understand the tradition, it was an honor to play for such a storied franchise."

Davis was born in Live Oak, Florida, and attended Suwannee High School, where he was a four-year starter on the Suwannee Bulldogs football team.

His senior season in 1996 was his best. He was captain for both the football and basketball teams, and was also a first-team Florida Class 4A all-state selection, and a SuperPrep high school All-American in football.

Notes on Andra Davis

Years Played: 2002–2008
Position: Linebacker
Height: 6'1"
Weight: 250
Hometown: Live Oak, FL
Current Residence: Aurora, CO
Occupation: Owns a motivational speaking and educational company, "All Roads Open"
Accomplishments: Attended Suwannee High School, where he was the captain of both the football and baseball teams his senior season. Was a first-team All-SEC selection and a second-team All-American in his senior season in Florida. Was a Super-Prep high school All-American in football. Played in 143 career NFL games over ten seasons, this after being a 2002 fifth-round pick of the Browns. He recorded 786 tackles, 12 sacks, and nine interceptions during his career with the Browns, Broncos, and Bills. He posted 100-plus tackles in three of his first five seasons in Cleveland and received the Bills' Ed Block Courage Award in 2011, which is given to players who exemplify inspiration, sportsmanship, and courage, as decided by their teammates. Graduated with a bachelor's degree in social sciences at UNLV in 2012. The father of three daughters: Alisha, 15; Amber, 12; and Andrea, 9.
Nickname: None

Following high school, Davis attended the University of Florida, where as a junior in 2000 he played on the Gators' SEC Championship team.

In his 35 games at Florida, he was the starter for 23 of them and ended his career with 232 tackles, five sacks, and four forced fumbles.

Despite his solid career at Florida, where in his senior season he was also a first-team All-SEC selection and a second-team All-American, he lasted till the fifth round of the 2002 NFL Draft, something that always seemed to bother Davis.

"I felt like I had a lot to prove that year. And every year," Davis said.

"I felt that I should have been drafted earlier. I went fifth round, but I knew I was better than that, so I felt like I had a lot to prove. It's easy to go out there and prove people wrong when you feel that you've been robbed, and also when you have responsibilities."

The Browns' 2002 season saw the team go 9–7, good enough for their only playoff appearance. Davis played in all 16 games but never got a start.

Heading into 2003, the team was in a transition at the linebacker spot, trying to add young players while still having them battle with veterans for playing time. Davis was in the mix for some of that playing time.

"I was named the starter during camp, but it happened late," Davis recalls of training camp 2003.

"They had brought in Barry Gardner from Philly that year. He was a true professional. We competed, but at the same time he helped me and showed me what it was like to be a professional."

Davis needed to stand out to become a starter entering 2003, and, while competing with others on the roster, he was finally able to make an impact.

"It was late in the camp and I remember talking to Chaun Thompson, and me and B.G. were battling for the position on who was going to be the starting linebacker, and knowing I had a child on the way I told Chaun, 'Man, I gotta do something,' Davis said.

"After we had that conversation I went out and had a really good practice, and finished it up with a really good preseason game.

"It was the third preseason game where most of the so-called starters play, and ever since then it was a wrap."

Much was expected from the Browns in 2003. With the team coming off a narrow loss to Pittsburgh in the playoffs, people felt the Browns were an up-and-coming team ready to turn the corner.

For Davis, that opening day against a future Hall of Fame quarterback was a special one.

The Game

I was fortunate enough to have a bunch of big games individually. But I would just say my first NFL start against the Indianapolis Colts and Peyton Manning.

The opener in 2003. My daughter was born the next day, so there was a lot going on.

We knew that it was my first NFL start, but at the same time my wife was about to have my second child, the next day or any minute.

So I will always remember that time. Those two days were great. We lost to the Colts, 9–6, but to hold Peyton Manning to nine points, I thought that was a huge feat for three incoming second-year starters.

The Browns had just got rid of all their veteran players the year before, so no one really knew what was gonna happen. But we did know that we had to go out there and leave it all out on the field.

No one knew what was going to happen with three new starters, especially at the linebacker spot.

Our three young linebackers, myself included, were all making their first NFL starts.

All eyes were on us. People thought we were going to get blown out. The Colts had Edgerrin James, the running back. Manning at quarterback.

Marvin Harrison and Reggie Wayne at wide receiver, and for us to go out there and hold them to three field goals, that gave us a lot of confidence to know that if we held them to nine points, we were able to go out and compete with anybody.

It was different because a couple other linebackers, Ben Taylor and Kelvin Bentley, were already penciled in as starters early in the spring. I was the last one to be named starter.

I felt I was more mature because I had a kid already and a kid on the way, and was married. So my personal life was simpler than theirs.

They were more into going out and I was a family guy. I was either at work or at home. So it was a lot easier in that aspect, but it was also more pressure on me because I had more responsibilities than them, so I just knew I had to do more.

I always felt I was a natural leader. I'm the type of guy to say what's on my mind, but I always try to lead by example, as well.

Playing against Manning was a huge thrill, and a great challenge. During that time he was basically in the prime of his career. He was definitely Hall of Fame caliber from day one all the way through.

I remember the game was tied, and it was late in the fourth quarter. They got the ball, and they put together a final drive to end up kicking a field goal to win the game.

During that last drive, I remember we had a couple of opportunities to get off the field, but we didn't. And they made the plays.

They showed why they were as good as they were. They didn't panic under pressure. The DawgPound was rockin' that day.

The Colts just did what they did. They took care of their business. They didn't fold, and just played good ball.

The Aftermath

The Browns' 2003 season was a tough one. Coming off the playoff season in 2002, the team went 5–11, and after sitting at 3–3 after six games the team went 2–8 in their final ten contests.

The team lost 11 games overall but suffered just four blowouts in those 11 setbacks. Davis recalls how hard the team fought in '03 but just were not able to close out games.

"It was very rarely that someone just beat us really bad," Davis said.

"We just could never get the ball to bounce our way. We could never do something to make the extra play. It seemed like my whole career in Cleveland the teams were just that same way. Even the year that we went 10–6, we missed the playoffs. It's like 'Come on. What more do we have to do?'"

Davis was a part of the 2007 team that was one bad late season loss in Cincinnati away from making the postseason and then moved on after the 2008 season.

He spent the 2009 season in Denver with the Broncos and then played his final two years in Buffalo with the Bills before retiring after the 2011 campaign.

Today he is back in Colorado, living in the beautiful city of Aurora and running his own business called "All Roads Open," helping others become better people.

"I do a lot of mentoring and public speaking. Just giving back to the kids. To motivate them to do better than I did. AllRoadsOpen. org," Davis said.

"It's a non-profit organization; we do a lot of community service and giving back. I have three daughters. My oldest plays basketball, and my two youngest play soccer. It's non-stop, so now I'm like Davis taxi cab. I live about eight minutes from the Broncos' facility in Aurora, Colorado."

Davis built himself up from a player who should have been drafted sooner to one whom Browns fans embraced during his time with the franchise.

He still thinks about his time with the Browns, and has great respect for the fans and organization that made him a name player on teams that just couldn't get over the hump.

"For me to work my way up and become a household name in Cleveland, I wish I could have finished my career there, but it was just great, a great time for me, and I loved everything about being in Cleveland," Davis said.

"I wish we would have won more, but even through the losses I would not have wanted to go through that with anyone else than with the guys that I played with in Cleveland. Everybody truly cared."

It's rare for a former Browns player to not mention the fans, and how no matter the weather, the record, or circumstances, for them to come out week after week.

Davis himself is included in the list of former Browns who loved the fans who would turn out week after week and show up at the stadium on Sunday, ready to cheer on the brown and orange.

"Every week those fans were there; they were loyal," Davis remembers.

"Cleveland is a blue collar, hard-working town, and they know that if you are doing your best, that's all that they really expect. They were disappointed when we lost, but if they know you gave everything you had, then they would respect you for that."

CHAPTER 3

MATT STOVER

Kicker 1991–1995
The Game: November 6, 1994, vs New England Patriots at
Cleveland Stadium
CLEVELAND BROWNS 13—NEW ENGLAND PATRIOTS 6

WHEN FORMER CLEVELAND Browns kicker Matt Stover took the field and wound up pointing to the sky, it almost always meant something good had just happened.

It was Stover's signature trademark, something he did a lot converting 108 of 134 field goals in the five years he played for the Browns.

Stover has the distinction of being the "last" true Browns player ever in terms of transitioning from one franchise to another.

He went with the team to Baltimore in 1996 and played for the Ravens for 13 seasons, all the way till 2008.

No other player who left Cleveland with the first regime of the Browns for Baltimore played nearly that long.

"People say to me all the time how I was the last remaining Brown for 13 years after the move, and how incredible it was," Stover recalls.

Born in Dallas, Texas, in January of 1968, Stover played his high school ball at Lake Highlands High School in Dallas.

Oddly enough, another former Browns kicker attended the same high school, that being Phil Dawson, who kicked for the Browns from 1999 to 2012.

GAME OF MY LIFE: CLEVELAND BROWNS

Notes on Matt Stover

Years Played: 1991–1995
Position: Kicker
Height: 5'11"
Weight: 178
Hometown: Dallas, TX
Current Residence: Baltimore, MD
Occupation: Public Speaker for Financial Institutions and Runs the Players' Philanthropy Fund
Accomplishments: Took home All-District honors as both a wide receiver and kicker playing for Lake Highlands High School in Dallas, Texas. During the 1985-'86 season he converted a 53-yard field goal. At Louisiana Tech, hit 64 of 88 field goals in his four years, also punted as a senior 36 times, averaging 34.1 yards per punt. Earned All-Conference honors in 1989. Was placed in the Louisiana Tech Hall of Fame in 2011. Scored 2,004 points in NFL career, hitting 471 of 563 field goals, 83.7 percent. Hit a career-long field goal of 55 yards. Was a two-time Pro Bowl kicker, two-time AFC Champion, and two-time Super Bowl champion. Won the PFW Golden Toe Award in 2000 and also was placed in the Baltimore Ravens Ring of Honor. Dad to two college athletes who both play lacrosse.
Nickname: None

Browns kicker Matt Stover (#3) with teammates Brian Kinchen and Brian Hansen during the 1992 season before a game at Cleveland Stadium. (Photo courtesy of Brian Kinchen.)

Stover won All-District honors as both a wide receiver and kicker at Lake Highlands, and during the 1985–86 LHHS season he kicked a 53-yard field goal, a sign of things to come in the pros.

After high school, Stover went on to graduate from Louisiana Tech, where he majored in marketing. He was very good in college, hitting on 64 of 88 field goal attempts.

He wasn't just a field goal kicker in college; he also punted and still holds the NCAA record for most punts in a single game with 16 back in 1988 against Louisiana-Monroe.

Stover was also a leader in college, where he was an active member and vice president of the Alpha Omega chapter of Delta Kappa Epsilon.

He was originally selected by the New York Giants in the 12th round of the 1990 NFL Draft, taken with the 329th overall pick.

The Giants won Super Bowl XXV in dramatic fashion over the Buffalo Bills, but Stover was watching as he spent the entire season on injured reserve.

The following season he inked a deal with the Browns, starting a career that he could never have imagined would last as long as it did.

He was coming in at the right time. A former Giants defensive coordinator, Bill Belichick, was taking over the Browns after they bottomed out the season before, going 3–13.

"Belichick I owe my career to," Stover recalls. "I know he wasn't really liked in Cleveland, but as he's proven he's a pretty darn good coach."

That first season, Stover hit on 16 field goals and racked up a total of 81 points as the Browns went 6–10. In 1992 the team went 7–9, and Stover again was a key, kicking the ball and accounting for 91 total points for the team.

The Browns were going through the normal growing pains, but the 1993 season was something no one would have expected.

The team started fast, winning five of their first seven games heading into a bye after a huge home win over the rival Pittsburgh Steelers.

The season took a sharp turn when Belichick, two weeks later and a day after a bad loss to the Denver Broncos, dumped its beloved quarterback Bernie Kosar, releasing the longtime signal caller.

The team seemed to play in a fog the rest of the year, winning just two of its final seven games and ending the year with the same 7–9 record they had the year before.

Through it all, Belichick was putting his stamp on the team, and while not many agreed with his moves, he was getting his guys in to rebuild a team that was 3–13 three years earlier.

"The last time the team had really won was 1989, and Bud Carson was the coach then, and he was fired the following year, and that's when Bill Belichick came in," Stover said.

"Belichick really cleaned house with the players that were there He had cut Bernie (Kosar) the year before in the middle of the season, and the fans were really calling for Belichick's head in 1993.

"I'll say this, Bill had a plan, and I was a part of that craziness."

The team surprised many in the NFL, starting quickly out of the gates with wins in six of their first seven games.

Stover was having his best season, and at 6–2 the Browns were set to host Belichick's former boss, Bill Parcells, and the New England Patriots in a big week-ten affair at Cleveland Stadium.

The Game

One of the games I recall vividly was in 1994; we played host to the New England Patriots at old Municipal Stadium in Cleveland.

We were in a race in the division with Pittsburgh, and with the win we got to 7–2. We had a city that was begging for a winner again.

The city was really behind us, finally, after everything that had happened in 1993, and even the media finally said, "Okay, looks like Belchick is for real and we've got us a team now."

It was a beautiful day but it was windy, so it was a hard game to kick in.

There were a couple things I remember about that game. Vinny Testaverde was down with an injury, and Mark Rypien was our quarterback.

Nick Saban was our defensive coordinator, and we had a really good defense that basically shut down Patriots quarterback Drew Bledsoe.

The winds that day were about 19 miles per hour, and what makes that stadium so different from the current stadium is that it was a wide baseball stadium. It was a big stadium but it sat low, so the air would come in there very differently.

The new stadium on the north side is a very steep stadium that really embraced the wind.

It still gets windy there. I had to kick a 52-yard game winner there at the new stadium, and it was a tough one, don't get me wrong, but not as tough as it would have been at the old stadium.

The wind tended to come out of the northeast and with the open end of the stadium where the Marlboro sign was, and that was a major issue that day as I can recall.

A more favorable wind was coming out of the northwest, so you had a little bit of play, but it was a really difficult stadium to kick in.

Plus there was another interesting factor about that game, and it's that the 1994 season was the first year the Browns were actually able to manage the field surface.

Vince Panarozi was the groundskeeper that Art Modell hired, and it was the first time that the Browns were actually able to manage the stadium, away from the Cleveland Stadium Authority.

It was a much better playing surface, even though it was painted dirt; it was a firm, painted dirt.

We had a defense that was stacked up with Saban running it; our offense was pretty much a run-orientated offense. Leroy Hoard was our lead back; he was doing a pretty good job.

We just had some momentum, we had confidence, and we had a great opportunity to have a good team and bring a winner back to Cleveland.

Unfortunately, we lost in the second round of the playoffs, and the following year we were doing decently well, and then the rug got pulled out underneath us with the move and we didn't play well much after that.

That 1994 season was a lot of fun, to be a part of a team that went through so much and to overcome so much change.

To be a part of that team and to help Cleveland experience a winner again was great.

The Aftermath

In 1994, the Browns were one of the surprise teams in the NFL. They ended the year 11–5, and qualified for the postseason and the right to host a wild card game.

"The 1994 year was kind of a turning point as I recall for that organization. We ended up losing the division to Pittsburgh, but we made the playoffs and ended up winning our first playoff game we played against New England," Stover recalls.

"We then in the divisional round went to Pittsburgh and got beat, which was a bummer of a deal; they started the game fast and it was over after that basically."

Things were looking good after the 1994 season, but little did the Browns players, the city, or pretty much anyone else know what was going to happen next.

"Going into 1995 we were stoked up; we really thought we had it. We knew we were a good team, we were rolling well," Stover said.

Art Modell announced in November of 1995 that the following year the team was moving to Baltimore, and that season would be the last in Cleveland.

The players felt the brunt of the wrath from fans, something that Stover remembers to this day, but he also knows it wasn't his or his teammates' fault.

"The players had nothing to do with the move," Stover said.

"With free agency, the salary cap, and the amount of money that was being paid to players, Art Modell for whatever reason, and I'm sure he had many of them, felt like it was best for him and his family to move the team.

"It ended up not being a bad deal financially for him, and Cleveland got a brand new team after three years. I was so happy that the colors and the records and everything stayed in Cleveland."

While things didn't end in a good way for the Browns and Stover, the 1994 season was a special one for the team as they made the Divisional round of the playoffs, something the team has yet to do since.

"The 1994 team, we really found ourselves, all the hard work had really paid off. We had a good, good formula, offensively we were good to a point, and defensively we were very strong," Stover said.

"1994 was the NFL's 75th anniversary, too, I recall that being a big deal, and we had a patch on our jersey, and that's the jersey I actually have framed in my basement.

"I have a big picture of my pointing up, I always pointed up good or bad, and it's of me in my Browns jersey in that 1994 season."

Stover went on to Baltimore with the team in 1996 and was the kicker on the team when they won the Super Bowl in 2000.

His career spanned an amazing 19 seasons, ending with five years with the Browns, 13 with the Ravens, and one two-game stint with the Indianapolis Colts.

His 471 field goals and 591 extra points added up to an amazing career for Stover, who always remembers with fondness the time with the Browns.

"Unfortunately, we ended up moving, but I will tell you what, it's a privilege of mine to have played there five years and then to be a part of that last team," Stover said.

Stover remained in Baltimore following retirement, raising his kids with his wife as well as running the Players' Philanthropy Fund, which helps players start their own charity foundations.

While many still think of Stover wearing purple as a Raven, he wouldn't have gotten there if not for his time with the Browns.

"A lot of the former guys, they say that Jonathan Ogden was the first Raven; my butt, it was all the Browns that moved there," Stover said.

"You look how things turn out, and how things happen, I played long enough my kids went all the way through high school.

"Both our kids were conceived in Cleveland, we lived in Strongsville, the first five years of our marriage was there, we really grew a lot, we really appreciated our time there."

CHAPTER 4

MICHAEL JACKSON

Wide Receiver 1991–1995
The Game: September 13, 1993, vs San Francisco 49ers at
Cleveland Stadium
CLEVELAND BROWNS 23—SAN FRANCISCO 49ERS 13

SAY THE NAME Michael Jackson, and you right away think of the deceased singer otherwise known as "The King of Pop."

Say the name Michael Jackson to Browns fans, and you come up with a totally different person.

From 1991 to 1995, Michael Jackson the football player, not the singer, ran routes for the Cleveland Browns as one of their leading wide receivers.

He caught 170 passes and scored 28 touchdowns during his five years with the Browns and was a speedster who make numerous big plays in big games.

Born in Tangipahoa, LA, on April 12, 1965, it didn't take long for Jackson to become a well-rounded athlete on the football field.

He attended Kentwood High School, where he played quarterback and free safety. He was all-state, and even played in the all-star game and was MVP of that game.

After a successful high school career, he decided to attend Southern Mississippi State, where he started as a quarterback, but eventually took a backseat at that position and moved to wide out.

For good reason.

Jackson was in the same position as Hall of Fame quarterback Brett Favre, and once the future three-time NFL MVP took over at

Notes on Michael Jackson

Years Played: 1991-1995
Position: Wide Receiver
Height: 6'4"
Weight: 195
Hometown: Tangipahoa, LA
Current Residence: Tangipahoa, LA
Occupation: Starting a Campaign to Run for Mayor of Tangipahoa, LA
Accomplishments: Played quarterback and free safety at Kentwood High School, and also was all-state and was the MVP of the All-Star game. Moved on to Southern Mississippi State, where he was teammates with Brett Favre, who eventually became the starting quarterback. Moved to wide out, where in three seasons caught 48 passes for 695 yards and seven scores. The Browns drafted him in the sixth round in 1991, the 141st overall pick. In his five seasons with the Browns, he started 49 of 69 games, catching 170 passes for 2,797 yards and 28 touchdowns. Caught ten passes for 169 yards in the team's two playoff games in 1994 against New England and Pittsburgh. After moving with the Browns to Baltimore as a member of the Ravens, had his best season in 1996. That year he caught 76 passes for 1,201 yards and 14 touchdowns. The following year caught 69 passes for 918 yards and four scores. Injures cut his career short, and he left the game after the 1998 season. In his career, caught 353 passes for 5,393 yards and 46 touchdowns.
Nickname: Thriller

quarterback at Southern Miss, Jackson knew he'd better look to play another spot on the field.

"Southern Miss brought me in as a quarterback, and they brought Brett in as a strong safety, yet he was given the opportunity to play quarterback in our freshman year," Jackson said.

"Our senior quarterback got injured, and Brett got the first opportunity to go into the game, and it was history from there. That's when in my sophomore year I moved to wide receiver.

"Then I injured my knee, so I didn't really get an opportunity till my junior year to play wide receiver, and then finally my senior year I focused in on it and started to accept it as the position I was going to play at that point."

The adjustment period for Jackson saw him go from four catches his sophomore season in which he hurt his knee, to 19 his junior year, and 25 his senior campaign.

He entered the NFL Draft in 1991, but due to his inexperience at the wide out spot, having just played it for three seasons, he felt that he would have to try to break into the league as a free agent.

Instead, the Browns were interested enough to make him a sixth-round pick, 141st pick overall, much to the surprise of Jackson.

"I thought it was my guys playing a joke on me, because I didn't think I was going to be drafted. I thought I would just get offers as a free agent to go somewhere," Jackson said.

"I think I hung the phone up the first time; I thought it was some of the guys that were at the training facility where I was.

"Then they called back, and it was the realization that it was really happening. Michael Lombardi and Ozzie were the two that called me."

Jackson started seven games his rookie season, the first for new head coach Bill Belichick, and pulled in 17 passes for 268 yards and a pair of touchdowns.

In his second season he started to be even more impactful, starting 14 games and making 47 catches for 755 yards and seven scores, as the Browns improved a game going from 6–10 the season before to 7–9.

It was that second season when Jackson finally started to feel as though he belonged at the wide out spot on an NFL roster.

"I went to Southern Miss as a quarterback, so when I got to the league I still hadn't learned to really be a receiver," Jackson said.

"My mentality wasn't at the wide receiver position yet, so I hadn't become a full-fledged receiver until my second year in the league."

Jackson did have the luxury of looking around at a roster with a plethora of good wide outs, catching passes from veteran leader Bernie Kosar.

He learned a lot those first two seasons, as the Browns continued to get better under Belichick.

"When you have the likes of Webster Slaughter, Brian Brennan, and Reggie Langhorne around, you tend to start to pick things up," Jackson remembers.

"I was a little different from all of them, so I was able to take a piece of each of them, and try to make myself, is what I was trying to do."

By 1993 Jackson was rounding into a go-to wide out on the Browns roster. He and the Browns were looking to take another step forward under Belichick, after a win at home in week one in which he caught seven passes and a touchdown.

Week two brought the Browns to the prime time spotlight, as they played on the national stage on Monday night football, taking on Steve Young, Jerry Rice, and the San Francisco 49ers.

The Game

The game that sticks out more than anything to me was in 1993, in the second week of the season we were hosting the San Francisco 49ers on Monday Night Football.

I remember telling our defensive backs, specifically Stevon Moore, if they were to shut Jerry Rice down, I would be the Jerry Rice of that night. I'll make the plays that people are expecting him to make.

Even though they were coming into Cleveland, we knew all the publicity was going towards Steve Young and Rice.

I told myself, "I don't want to hear all this Jerry Rice stuff, I'm going to be the Jerry Rice tonight," and that's the way I approached it.

I was actually able to go out there and perform so much, and how I think Jerry would have done, and that was just so grand for me.

We knew all of the hype was about San Francisco, Jerry Rice, Steve Young, Ricky Watters, just their history. When you look at them you think, "Who are we, we're just someone for them to come in and run over."

Bernie Kosar was our quarterback, and he was a seasoned vet, and you had a lot of youngsters on the team, so you had to have a seasoned vet to calm everybody down.

We'd be all hyped in the huddle and Bernie would get a hold of us and tell us, "Just calm down," and if you didn't calm down he'd really get into you.

That was a special thing, and just the belief that we had in Bernie, we knew that his physical ability wasn't the grandest of everything, but Bernie's mind substituted for his lack of ability in certain areas, and you never knew that he didn't have these abilities because of his mind and his knowledge of the game.

That's the thing that made everybody feel so good about playing with Bernie.

I caught a 35-yard touchdown in the game, and it was on our right sideline, and the Niners had Eric Davis covering me, and I kind of had to make a diving catch.

It was in the corner of the end zone, and it was amazing the feeling after you catch it. Again, you're a receiver, you're a receiver that doesn't have all of the confidence you need at that point, but there you are—the only game on in America, it's just so many emotions that go through your body.

I think I had dropped one earlier to where Bernie had slightly underthrown it, and I tried to grab it and go too fast, and I left it on my hip, so there were a lot of emotions tied up into that because I wanted to make up for that.

The Aftermath

The week two win over the Niners may have been the high point for the Browns in 1993. The team did get off to a 5–2 start after a key win over the rival Pittsburgh Steelers, helped out by a pair of punt returns by Eric Metcalf.

But the bottom dropped out two weeks later, as Bill Belichick and the team dumped quarterback Bernie Kosar the day after a loss to the Broncos, to drop to 5–3.

The season was never the same, as the team won just two more games the rest of the season and ended the year with the same 7–9 mark as the year before.

"That was a tough season," Jackson recalls, "and I'm saying even more so from a mental standpoint than from a physical, and that's what most people don't understand, this game carries a lot of mental weight." The release of Kosar sent the franchise into a complete tailspin and seemed also to totally divide the locker room at the same time.

"For the organization to take their franchise player basically and to bench him, what does that tell everyone else? Everybody's expendable," Jackson remembers.

"So now it's every man for himself, and I think that's where the division happened amongst the team. Now mentally it's every man for himself, it's not team anymore.

"Now the team is divided, and Bernie Kosar was just used as the example. I think that had a lot to do with it."

The media and fans were squarely against Belichick and what he was doing to their beloved players. The coach wanted to do things his way, and it didn't always sit well, not only with the players, but even more so with the fans and media.

"The Belichick that we as players knew, and the one that fans knew and the media knew, were totally different Belichicks," Jackson said.

"From a media standpoint it looked like me and Belichick had a problem because I was very outspoken, but there was such a respect for one another that the players had for him and he for the players, I don't think he was doing anything to try and instill that he was in control.

"I think that he wanted to win so bad, I think he felt he had to make some changes, and he needed to make some changes that people generally wouldn't like.

"He showed that he would be willing to make the changes that would be necessary in order to establish a winning franchise."

The team stayed behind Belichick, and it paid off in 1994 as the club came together to win 11 games, reaching the postseason for the first time since 1989.

They won a playoff game at home against New England before falling 29–9 to the Steelers in the divisional playoff round.

Things seemed to be on the upswing, but no one could have considered what would take place in 1995, as midway through the season owner Art Modell announced he was moving the franchise.

The team bottomed out after a 3–1 start, winning just two more games the entire season, ending their final year in Cleveland at 5–11, and on the way to Baltimore.

"That was another one of those mental toughness things, and it's not like we were not mentally tough already, but it was now like, 'Okay, what are we going to do?'" Jackson recalls.

"We knew that we were the ones that were going to get the brunt of the criticism, because we are the ones that are out there in the public, and they are going to be upset with us even though we didn't make the decision."

Jackson made the move to Baltimore with the rest of the Browns players who were still with the franchise. The team went 4–12, but the wide out had his best season as a pro, tying San Diego Chargers wide out Tony Martin for the most touchdowns in the NFL with 14.

"You were able to relax because you knew you were not going anywhere. It was a fresh start, it was an opportunity, and it almost felt like you were drafted all over again," Jackson said.

Injuries two seasons later ended Jackson's NFL career, one that spanned eight seasons between the Browns and Ravens, with 353 catches and 46 touchdowns.

His post-NFL career saw him move into the political field in his hometown of Tangipahoa in Louisiana, where he ran for public office and served as Mayor from 2008 to 2012.

He walked away from politics for a time but is starting a campaign to try to get back in office in the city he was born and raised in—Tangipahoa, LA.

Jackson's NFL career may be behind him, but he still takes time when he gets a fan letter from his glory days with the Browns to sign his name and send it back to the fans who loved him during his four-year stay in Cleveland.

"I still have people that send me mail, and I do my best to get it back out to them," Jackson said.

"Like I always tell the fans of the Cleveland Browns, if there was no support from them then there would be no reason for them to send me anything, so why wouldn't I take a moment to jot my name down and send it back to those people that made me relevant.

"Cleveland made me relevant."

CHAPTER 5

DON COCKROFT

Kicker 1968–1980
The Game: November 19, 1972, vs Pittsburgh Steelers at
Cleveland Stadium
CLEVELAND BROWNS 26—PITTSBURGH STEELERS 23

THE STORY OF this former Cleveland Browns kicker and punter
can be defined in two simple words: second chances.

His 13-year career with the Browns is filled with amazing memories and stories, none of which would have happened if not for Cockroft getting a number of second chances in life.

Born in Cheyenne, Wyoming, Cockroft went to a small high
school, Fountain Fort Carson High School, where he was a star in
three sports, lettering in all three.

"I jokingly tell people, you know we had 40 in our senior class and
35 of those were girls," Cockroft said. "That's probably why I was the
outstanding athlete my senior year."

His goal in high school was a simple one—to work hard and do
enough to earn a scholarship so that he could attend college.

He was willing to go the extra mile to try and get there, and started
kicking the football in order to give himself a good chance to get to
college.

"Basketball was my best sport, but obviously football was a big
part and I kicked," Cockroft said.

"I kicked from the seventh grade on because I happened to have
the strongest leg of anybody on our team. And so bottom line is, I

Notes on Don Cockroft

Years Played: 1968-1980
Position: Kicker
Height: 6'2"
Weight: 194
Hometown: Cheyenne, WY
Current Residence: Canton, OH
Occupation: Retired from the Mortgage Business, Author of the book *The 1980 Kardiac Kids*
Accomplishments: Was a three-sport star in high school in Colorado and lettered in all three sports, was also the starting quarterback and linebacker in high school. Was a walk-on at Adams State College, which is located in Colorado, and was a starter in the defensive backfield his senior season. Was selected by the Browns in the third round of the 1967 draft, with the 55th overall pick. Took over as Browns kicker in 1968 when Hall of Fame kicker-offensive tackle Lou Groza was waived by the team. Was the Browns punter for the first nine of his 13 seasons. Had an overall punting average of 40.3 in a career that saw him punt 651 times. Had a career-long punt of 71 yards. Made 65.9 percent (216 of 328) of his field goal attempts over his 13-year career. Ended his career with 1,080 points, playing in a total of 188 games, all with the Browns. Was the next-to-last "straight on" kicker in the NFL, the last being Mark Moseley.
Nickname: None

Browns safety Thom Darden and kicker Don Cockroft (r). (The Cleveland Press Collection)

wanted to go to college and I wanted to get a college education like my two older brothers were doing at that time, and thought I could get a scholarship actually to Colorado State University."

It wasn't to be for Cockroft going to Colorado State, so instead the first of many second chances happened in his life, as he ended up at Adams State College in Alamosa, Colorado.

"They contacted me and said if you come over and make the football team we will give you a scholarship. Which if I don't get a scholarship, my folks had no money I guess I don't go to college," Cockroft said.

It wasn't an easy road for Cockroft in college early on, since it didn't take very long for him to realize making the football team was no sure thing.

"I remember after ten days of three-a-day practices, not two-a-day, and realizing that 'Man, I'm not going to make this team,' and I remember calling my mom and crying and saying, 'Mom, I'm not going to make this team, can I come home?' and she flatly said, 'Donny, No.'

"She's also crying, and she basically said whatever you do son, don't quit. Said, 'Just do your best whatever it is, and see what happens.'

"It was then that I realized there's nobody kicking the ball, I don't think, around here any better than I can."

Cockroft worked at his craft at the kicking position, and eventually things started to turn around for him, as he was able to finally get a break due to all the hard work he did at the kicking position.

"Bottom line is, after practice I started to work on my kicking every day for 30 minutes, and made the varsity team as a kicker as a freshman, and led the nation my senior year with a 48-yard punting average," Cockroft said.

"If your name is at the top of the college punter list, they gotta look at you."

Cockroft had met his goal of making the team, and now it was time for another opportunity: to kick in the NFL.

He spent his time after college again looking for chances to impress as he got ready for the NFL Draft in 1967.

"I was playing a couple All-Star games, one I remember particularly was down in Miami, and I kicked a couple of field goals and punted well, and that's how the pros started to realize, 'Hey, this guy can kick,'" Cockroft said.

Things were going Cockroft's way, so on draft day he got a call from the Browns, a call that little did he know would set him up to replace a player who was one of the greatest in Browns franchise history.

"I was a third-round draft choice for the Browns and was brought in to replace the legendary Lou Groza," Cockroft said.

"What I didn't realize was what I was asked to do, and didn't realize he was thought of as a god as he was."

Cockroft was very good in his first season, hitting 18-of-24 field goals, but then the next three seasons he hit just barely over 50 percent of his field goals.

That led to the offseason of 1971, one that would change Cockroft's life forever. "I had some really tough decisions, one of them being can I play football and still be a Christian," Cockroft said.

"I led the NFL in field-goal percentage my rookie season, and overall I had a great rookie season," Cockroft said.

"1969, '70, and '71 I really wasn't that good; they had drafted another kicker, George Hunt, out of Tennessee in 1972 in the fifth round, and I thought it was to replace me as a kicker and I would stay on as a punter.

"I was very confused and frustrated after those three seasons, and I wanted to honor God, but I was also thinking how people didn't want to hear from someone who was failing."

Cockroft, not sure of his future after the Browns drafted kicker George Hunt from Tennessee in the fifth round of the 1971 NFL Draft, went back home to Colorado, where he enrolled in Bible college, looking to find that inner peace.

"The reason was to find an answer, what am I missing spiritually? God, how can I honor you if I'm failing?"

"God really showed and opened my heart. Jesus said in Luke 9:23 to deny thyself, and I had come to the conclusion that I hadn't really denied myself, and I didn't want to give up football," Cockroft said.

"In 1971, I really surrendered football and everything to God. I got a call from the Billy Graham crusade, which was having an event in Cleveland, and they asked if I would share my testimony. My thought was, 'Wow, I'm probably done with the Browns, but what a way to leave Cleveland.'"

Cockroft spoke that night to the over 40,000 people at the crusade, but instead of his career with the Browns being over, a new special teams coach, Al Tabor, came in and helped Cockroft get back to the high percentage ways and regain the Browns' place-kicking duties.

"I could kick the ball, but I was finally at peace with myself and surrendering to God in peace, and I could do what I was, and not out of fear but just out of just doing it," Cockroft said.

"I remained the Browns' punter and kicker in 1972, and it would have been without question my best year as a Cleveland Brown player in 1972.

"We're having a really good season, Mike Phipps is our quarterback that year, and obviously the Steelers and Houston both have very good football teams, and we're not supposed to be in the race but we're still having a good season."

On a four-game win streak at 6–3, the Browns got set for one of their biggest games of 1972, a huge home showdown with the rival Steelers at the stadium.

The Game

Pittsburgh comes to Cleveland in November of 1972. They're up by two games, and with the 14-game schedule there's four games left. The game was November 19, 1972.

There were 83,000 people at that stadium that day, and it was rainy, nasty, and we're not supposed to beat the Steelers.

We go out ahead of the Steelers at halftime, it was 20 to 10, and then I kicked my third field goal in the third quarter and we're leading the game, 23–10.

I remember the locker room at halftime, and we're pumped, we're excited and we're going to go out and beat these guys.

We don't ever beat the Steelers, you know, so this is huge for us.

We're leading the game 23–10, and they come back and get to 23–17, and then Franco Harris goes 75 yards for a touchdown in the fourth quarter, and they get the lead on us at 24–23.

Now we're down, and then we have to score again to try and get the lead to try and win this game.

I've already kicked three field goals in the mud that day, so I'm feeling pretty good about myself, but I'm hoping we would just score a touchdown in the last two minutes.

We're down, 24–23, and I go out and attempt a 26-yard field goal to win the game. I go out and pray, "Lord, help me," and there's a lot of pressure here.

I'll never forget I went through all the rules, keep your head down, step straight, and I went to kick it and disobeyed the most important rule in kicking and lifted my head up.

We're at the open end of the stadium, and that ball missed by two inches to the right.

It was quieter at the "Red Right 88" game, but at that point it was so silent. I was devastated. I had given up on football and gave up the game, and I'm having the best season of my life.

I go out there and miss the most important kick of my life. I'm ready to die, I just couldn't believe it.

I remember Billy Andrews, one of our linebackers, when I hit the sideline he saw my face and said, "Don, get your head up; we're going to get the ball back and give you a second chance."

So they get the ball and we stop them. I remember on third down Jerry Sherk and Billy Andrews sacking Terry Bradshaw on third down.

They had to punt, and we got the ball back with like 49 seconds left. I again prayed, "Lord, this time I'll keep my head down."

I know it sounds selfish, but then another guy came over and said, "Don, you know you're going to get another chance at this, right?"

So, bottom line is we stopped them and Mike Phipps came in and hit a couple unbelievable passes slipping and sliding in the mud, and with 13 seconds left on the clock, I find myself back out on that field.

What is amazing is, the ball was within three to five inches of where it was two minutes earlier. Almost the identical spot.

Of course the snap, the hold, everything was perfect, except this time I kept my head down, and drove through the ball, and when I looked up I saw heaven, because that ball sailed dead center through the uprights.

The fact is that I got that second chance, the fact is that we did win that game, and then went on to have a really good season.

It was all about the second chance, the fact that The Lord gives us two, three, even four chances. I probably have 15 games that have a story that I can relate more than just football to.

We won, and it was a pivotal game for us because we were the wild card team that year.

The Aftermath

The 1972 Browns played the undefeated Miami Dolphins in the wild-card game that season in Miami, and despite how good the Dolphins had been, the Browns hung with them most of the day.

In the end, a couple of key mistakes were the Browns' undoing, and they lost, 20–14, to the eventual Super Bowl champions, still the only undefeated team in NFL history.

"We came as close to anybody to beating Miami that year; they beat us, 20–14, and their first touchdown came when they blocked a punt of mine," Cockroft said.

"So they scored a touchdown on a blocked punt, and we had five interceptions that day, yet they beat us by just six points.

"Just to be a part of what they did, there was something very special about it. We could have beat them."

The 1972 season was a true turning point in the life of Cockroft in a number of ways. He stuck as the Browns' kicker for another eight seasons before he was released during camp in 1980 and eventually retired.

He left the game with a solid 13-year career with the Browns, hitting 65.9 percent on field goals, and ending his career with 216 field goals.

His story is unique; it's all about not giving up, as well as identifying and taking advantage of those important second chances.

"It's the idea of the second chance, and I was given far more of a second chance to come closer to our Lord and Savior," Cockroft said.

"I was a kid from Adams State College, Fountain Fort Carson High School; I was just so overwhelmed, I think that's why I just didn't make it."

In the end, though, Cockroft's career was filled with plenty more makes than misses, something that Browns fans will always appreciate about the kicker.

CHAPTER 6

FELIX WRIGHT

Safety 1985–1990
The Game: October 26, 1987, vs Los Angeles Rams at
Cleveland Stadium
CLEVELAND BROWNS 30—LOS ANGELES RAMS 17

NOTHING HAS EVER been easy for former Browns safety Felix Wright.

From being undrafted to teaching physical education and history, playing in the CFL, to finally making it to the NFL, Wright has worked for everything in becoming a success.

Wright played for the Browns from 1985 to 1990, having a big part of the glory years of the team as they made it to three AFC Title games in 1986, '87, and '89.

Just like in getting there, it took some time to be a starter and make an impact, but once he did he was able to be a big part of the Browns' defense that helped the team make it to within one step of the Super Bowl.

"I didn't really know what I was in for when I came to Cleveland from Hamilton, Ontario, because I was playing in the CFL," Wright said.

"I'm sure plenty of the guys probably feel similar, in that I played for the CFL, and we had quite a few guys come from the USFL, and Bernie (Kosar) came from the supplemental draft."

That group of guys became the best team for a few years during the mid-to late 1980s in the AFC, and at the forefront of the group was head coach Marty Schottenheimer.

Notes on Felix Wright

Years Played: 1985–1990
Position: Safety
Height: 6'2"
Weight: 190
Hometown: Carthage, MO
Current Residence: Westlake, OH
Occupation: Financial Advisor to NFL Players
Accomplishments: His 1971 Little League team was Missouri State Champion. Was a three-sport star in high school, playing and lettering in baseball, basketball, and football. In his senior year in high school was both all-conference and all-district honors in football, and also was named the most determined and inspirational athlete on the baseball team. His number 15 at Carthage High School was retired in tribute to his athletic accomplishments. At Drake played in every game all four years, and also was team captain and MVP as a senior. Playing in the CFL for Hamilton, made the 1984 CFL All-Star team, and in the 1984 Grey Cup intercepted two passes. Came to the Browns in 1985 and played in 32 games his first two seasons, not starting a game, and then in 1987 played in every game, staring seven and picking off four passes. In 1989 led the NFL in interceptions with nine and was named the Most Valuable Player on the Browns. Played two more seasons with the Minnesota Vikings in 1991 and 1992, and wrapped up his NFL career in Kansas City in 1993.
Nickname: Mr. Monday Night

Former Browns safety Felix Wright enjoying life after the NFL. (Courtesy of Felix Wright)

"We all came together from different areas of the draft and free agency, and we didn't know that Marty Schottenheimer would put together the team that he did," Wright recalls.

"It was obvious he knew what he wanted to do, and did exactly what he wanted to do with the team. You could just tell the chemistry we had with that team, we were all such good friends, we all hung out together.

"It was an 'all for one and one for all' kind of group."

Wright was born in Carthage, Missouri, and in high school he lettered in football, baseball, and basketball.

He played his college ball at Drake and never missed a game in his four years at the school. He was team captain and MVP as a senior, but went undrafted and took a job as a teacher in Missouri.

Wright, though, never gave up on football; he played three years for the Hamilton Tiger Cats of the CFL. A highlight moment for Wright was during the Grey Cup, when he picked off two passes.

He arrived in Cleveland and fought his way onto the roster, and became part of a team and culture that took over the city as the team made run after run at the Super Bowl.

"The fan base was pretty awesome; they were pretty awesome before we even came there," Wright said. "They had the 'Kardiac Kids' to entertain them before we came along.

"When Hanford Dixon and Frank Minnifield came up with the 'Dawg Pound,' it took on a life of its own, and it was pretty crazy how that took off. It made the fans even more enthusiastic about what we were doing for the city of Cleveland."

After the team wasn't able to overcome the Denver Broncos in the 1986 AFC Title Game, the Browns could have been thrown for a loop in 1987.

The league's players went on strike, stopping games in week three, and the NFL brought in replacement players to play weeks four through six.

Wright and the rest of the Browns sat on the sidelines, keeping in playing shape and waiting to be able to take the field again to try and continue their run to a hopeful Super Bowl.

The strike finally ended after week six, and the NFL players got back to work. The Browns' first game back was a career changer for Wright, who used the night as a stepping stone in his NFL career.

The Game

My signature game had to be a Monday night game in 1987. We were coming off the players' strike, and we were playing the Los Angeles Rams.

At that point in my career I was kind of a 'tweener,' where I was in and out of the lineup, but that night I had a big night, two interceptions, one of which went for a touchdown.

I never looked back after that game; I was a starter the remainder of my career, and that was kind of my signature game because it got me in the starting lineup, and it was just an awesome feeling.

Being a starter beginning with that night helped me go on to leading the league in 1989 in interceptions, which is kind of a dream for me because you always want to be the top guy at your position in the league, and I accomplished that leading the league in interceptions.

That was kind of cool; that was probably my best year in terms of productivity, as a ball player.

The crowd that night was just so electric, and back in those days we played in the old stadium, and it sat over 80,000 people, and we put over 80,000 people in there each and every week.

Back in the day, the NFL as far as being on TV wasn't like what it is today, where pretty much everyone in the country gets to see every team.

Pretty much the Cleveland area used to get to see the Cleveland teams; fans in the east and west coast really didn't get to see us very much, they used to just get to see their own teams.

So when you got a chance to play on national television, when you played on a Monday night, it was a real hyped game.

I think today it's still like that, where players excel and play better when they are playing in front of a national crowd instead of just in front of a regional crowd.

You have a lot more incentive when you know your family is watching, and more people are watching. It shouldn't really be like that but it is.

It just so happens that I had a little bit of luck going my way, and it seems like when we played on Monday nights I always seemed to come up with a big turnover for my team.

That's why Marty Schottenheimer nicknamed me "Mr. Monday Night," because I was fortunate to always seem to make a play on Monday night, so the nation could see.

The first interception I had that night, the Rams were driving for a touchdown and they had a running back, Charles White, and he kind of chased me down, and it was a foot race.

I picked it off at the goal line and raced it 68 yards, and Charles White, who was with the Browns at one point, ended up making a shoestring tackle on me.

The next one, it was just a down and in route, and I remember we had seen it in film, and we knew the down and distance and that it was time to come.

I was able to make a play on it in front of Henry Ellard and take it in 40 yards for a touchdown to build the score that we had, and at the time it made it 17–0.

That game was an exciting one because at the time the Rams had Eric Dickerson, as well, who was a fantastic running back, so they had a decent team, but we were the team back then.

We were favored, and we did what we were supposed to do; we were supposed to win that game and we ended up doing it.

Coming off the strike you just never know how the guys are going to be. You know, they were out six weeks and you had to wonder if they were going to come back and be in shape, or not in shape, and we were hoping the replacement players wouldn't bang up our record too much.

Thankfully, they only lost one game, so we were in pretty good shape, and we took care of business in that game and just took it from there.

I think we persevered pretty well. Anytime you go through a strike at any level it's a tough situation because everybody has their own story, and their own situation.

We had some guys cross the line, and sometimes with that it brings animosity, but I just tried to look at it with an open mind, and think "this guy's situation might be different from mine," and this might be the reason he did cross the line.

It gave you something to think about, but I think we got something accomplished—to each their own.

You have a bunch of individuals that make a team, and during that strike I don't know if it brought us more together, but we did have a couple practices where we were able to check up on each other and make sure we were staying in shape.

We knew eventually we would be going back in to play real games.

The Aftermath

The Browns' season ended with a mark of 10–5, a game better than the Houston Oilers, and with them as winners of the AFC Central.

The team dispatched the Indianapolis Colts in the AFC Divisional Round, 38–21, at home, and it set up a second straight AFC Title Game against the Denver Broncos, only this time it would be in Mile High Stadium.

The game forever remembered as "The Fumble" saw the Browns rally from being down, 21–3, at halftime, to tying the game, 31-all, in the fourth quarter.

The Browns' end, though, came that day as they couldn't hold NFL MVP and Broncos QB John Elway in check, and after going down, 38–31, in the fourth quarter, they drove down the field for what they felt would be the tying score.

It wasn't to be, as Earnest Byner fumbled near the goal line, and the Browns walked off the field in Denver a loser, 38–33.

To this day, Wright recalls that, as well as the 1989 AFC Title Game loss, with the same disappointment that many Browns fans still do.

"It's a bummer; it comes up every year pretty much around the same time, and since Denver just won the Super Bowl they always seem to bring up those games with Elway," Wright said.

"It is a bummer to think about it, actually. I was there four times; I played in four AFC Championship games and got beat that game and was not able to make it to the Super Bowl, and it's tough."

Wright went on after leaving the Browns in 1991 to play two seasons with the Minnesota Vikings and then in 1993 played with the Kansas City Chiefs before retiring.

"I would have done anything to play in a Super Bowl. That was a dream to do that one day and get that accomplished; I think that's everybody's dream," Wright said.

Now, over 20 years later, Wright still deals with football players, but on a whole other level. He runs a group that handles players' finances, and teaches players how to save some today for their future.

He still connects with Browns fans often and recalls with good memories the times walking onto the field at old Cleveland Stadium in front of over 80,000 fans.

"The fan base was great, and I think that's part of the reason why, when you have players when they do retire, they retire in the city, because the city treated them so well," Wright said.

"I've brought my two kids up in Cleveland, and they love the city, as well."

CHAPTER 7

STEVE HEIDEN

Tight End 2002–2009
The Game: December 29, 2002, vs Atlanta Falcons at Browns Stadium
CLEVELAND BROWNS 24—ATLANTA FALCONS 16

BORN AND RAISED in the blue collar state of Minnesota, known for its beautiful lakes and cold winters, Steve Heiden was a perfect fit as tight end for the Cleveland Browns.

Heiden played eight seasons in Cleveland, most of them ending up with a number of more losses than wins, but not because of a lack of effort and heart.

"My time in Cleveland was great for me. I really enjoyed my time with the organization, as well as being a part of the city," Heiden said.

A native of Rushford, Minnesota, Heiden was born September 21, 1976.

He played his high school ball at Rushford-Peterson, pulling in 201 catches and scoring 14 touchdowns, then moving on to play his college ball at South Dakota State.

In his college years, Heiden had 112 total grabs for 1,499 yards and eight scores, while spending his study time majoring in early childhood education.

The tight end got the call from the San Diego Chargers in the third round of the 1999 NFL Draft.

Joining San Diego, Heiden made his NFL debut in week five and in three seasons played in 42 games in San Diego for the Chargers, starting 13 games.

Notes on Steve Heiden

Years Played: 2002–2009
Position: Tight End
Height: 6'5"
Weight: 275
Hometown: Rushford, MN
Current Residence: Phoenix, AZ
Occupation: Arizona Cardinals Assistant Coach
Accomplishments: Caught 201 passes for 1,689 yards and 14 touchdowns in high school at Rushford-Peterson in Rushford, Minnesota. At South Dakota State in four years had 112 total grabs for 1,499 yards and eight touchdowns. Was the 69th pick overall (third round) of the San Diego Chargers in the 1999 NFL Draft. In three seasons with the Chargers, caught 14 passes for 87 yards and two scores. Caught his first pro pass in week four of the 2000 season against the Seahawks. First touchdown came in week 15 of the same season in a loss to the Panthers. Was moved to the Browns following the 2001 season and played eight years with Cleveland, playing in a total of 106 games with 70 starts. In his time with the Browns, had 187 catches for 1,602 yards and 12 scores. Became an assistant coach with the Arizona Cardinals on February 5, 2013, joining the staff of former Browns offensive coordinator Bruce Arians.
Nickname: None

Before the 2002 season, Heiden was moved to the Browns, and while moving from San Diego to Cleveland might not sound like a great move to most, Heiden welcomed the shift.

"I was drafted by San Diego, played three seasons there, and then was traded to Cleveland. Being in Cleveland felt more like home to me, being a Minnesota kid," Heiden said.

Heiden fit in right away, and that 2002 season was a special one for the Browns, as it was the season they made their only postseason trip since their return to the NFL.

"It seemed like in 2002 and 2007 you really could tell what Cleveland could be like as a football town," Heiden said. "Those two seasons when we were winning games, there was nothing like it being in Cleveland; it was amazing.

"When the Browns are winning, there's nothing else like it as a player, being around and walking around that city when the team is good is just great," Heiden recalled.

When Heiden got to Cleveland, the team was coming off a 7–9 campaign, the first for new head coach Butch Davis.

The Browns seemed ready to make a push forward in 2002, and Heiden was happy to be a part of the ride for a young up-and-coming team.

"I really didn't have a grasp on it when I got there," Heiden said. "We knew we could play with any team in the league, we were winning games. We had a really good group of coaches, and that season was just a blast."

As everything with the Browns, things in 2002 didn't exactly come easy. The team started 2–4, before winning four of their next five.

The club sat at 7–7, with two critical games left if they were going to make the playoffs.

They rallied for a win in Baltimore in week 15 and came home to host budding superstar Michael Vick and the Atlanta Falcons in week 16.

The Game

There's a lot of games that come to mind when it came to playing with the Browns, but the one that was most like a home playoff game was the game in the 2002 season against Atlanta.

That was the game I can look back on and say it was most like a home playoff game. The fans, the excitement, even the weather that day. It was a great atmosphere.

That day against Michael Vick and the Falcons, we played a really good game against a really good team. A playoff team that had a superstar player in Vick.

I remember the week leading up, and the practices that Butch Davis used to run. The one thing that stands out was, it wasn't a big pressure thing to us.

We knew what we were doing, and at that point it was late in the season, and we had already won eight games, and were coming off a huge win the week before on the road against the Ravens.

It was pretty much a given, if we beat the Falcons, that we were going to the playoffs, but at the same time we didn't put a lot of pressure on ourselves to go out and do anything we hadn't done before.

My perspective as a tight end was to come out and just kick their ass, and that's what I felt we were able to do.

We felt if we just played our game we would get the job done. We came out, we played hard, and we got the "W" to get to the playoffs.

That game against Atlanta didn't exactly start out as we planned, though, as we lost our quarterback Tim Couch on the first play of the second quarter and had to turn to Kelly Holcomb, but we were determined not to let that stop us.

Tim had really been playing well that season. he had led us down the field for that win the week before against the Ravens, and it was tough to see him have to leave that game.

I remember, though, how much confidence Kelly had; he was the most confident guy in the locker room.

If there's one thing about Kelly it's that he's got a certain swagger and a great amount of confidence in himself, so we knew when he took the field he would get the job done, and he did.

I myself didn't really have much of a game stat wise; I caught two passes for nine yards, but what I do remember was having a big game blocking for our top running back, Willliam Green.

Willie had a big day to help out our offense. He ran for over 170 yards, and early in the second quarter he had a touchdown to put us up, 10–0.

They kind of came back on us, and by the fourth quarter they were ahead, 16–10. We got a touchdown from Kelly to Kevin Johnson to take the lead, and then the play that everyone seems to remember with Willie to help us extend the lead.

I don't remember the exact play call; funny enough, I'll bet (current Arizona Cardinals and then Browns offensive coordinator) Bruce Arians still does.

It was a run to the right, and I remember seeing Willie get into the open, and he was gone. It was pretty exciting, and we felt we were in a pretty good position after that.

Our defense had to make a late stand to keep us ahead. I recall Vick got them down the field pretty quick, and then they had the ball inside our five in the final minute.

I was standing on the opposite sideline and was standing next to my teammate Aaron Shea, and they got down to the one with still over a minute left.

It seemed like every second was taking a half hour. Our defense, though, came through, and the game ended with them on our one with us celebrating.

I remember leaving the field and being so pumped, knowing that our season was going to continue.

The Aftermath

The long run by Green that put the Browns ahead by eight is still one of the highlights of the team since their return to the NFL in 1999.

The clip is often played with the famous call by Browns radio voice Jim Donovan, who excitedly shouted out "Run, Willie, run," as the play was going on.

The win pushed the Browns into the postseason as the number six seed and set up a wild third matchup with the rival Pittsburgh Steelers, who had beaten the Browns twice in the 2002 season, both times by three points.

With Couch done for the year and Holcomb stepping in, many felt it would be easy for the home team Steelers to get past the Browns and move on to the divisional round.

Little did they know that Holcomb, who had just three NFL starts under his belt to that point, would have the breakout game of his career, throwing for 429 yards and three scores.

The game, though, will be remembered for the huge letdown by the Browns after they built a 24–7 second-half lead.

The team's defense couldn't hold the lead, and Pittsburgh rallied for a devastating 36–33 win that ended the Browns' season.

Heiden's career with the Browns continued for seven more seasons, until he left the game in 2011.

His most memorable game that many recall came in 2004 when, in a 58–48 shootout loss to the Bengals, he pulled in three touchdowns to go along with seven catches for 82 yards.

Heiden started 70 games in his eight-year career with the Browns, playing in a total of 109. In his time with the Browns, he totaled 187 catches for 1,602 yards and 14 touchdowns.

He played on the two most successful Browns teams since their return in the NFL in 1999, playing on that 2002 team, as well as the 2007 team that went 10–6, missing the postseason by a game.

"The 2007 season was kind of odd. We got beat bad in the opener at home by the Steelers, and we had to really regroup. The day after we lost to Pittsburgh we traded our starting quarterback, Charlie Frye, which was kind of an odd move," Heiden recalls.

"Derek Anderson was named our starter, and things quickly got better for us. He had, and we had, a lot of confidence in him. In 2006 we went 4–12, and I don't think people really expected anything out of us in 2007, but in that locker room we knew we were not a 4–12 or 5–11 football team."

The 2007 Browns had a high-powered offense, and a defense that played well enough to keep the team in games.

They found themselves at 9–5 and had what was deemed a "make-or-break" game with the Bengals in Cincinnati in the second-to-last week of the season.

With winds gusting, the team wasn't able to take advantage of its high-powered passing game and were stunned by Cincinnati, 19–14.

"That season we had a real group of guys and we wound up winning ten games, and didn't even make the playoffs. It really came down to one game, and late in the season we went down to Cincinnati, and just didn't get the job done," Heiden said.

"It was a shame; we were a really good team that season, and it would have been fun to see what we would have done in the playoffs, but we just didn't get the job done."

Heiden wrapped up his playing career with a total of 202 catches for 1,689 yards and 14 touchdowns playing for the Chargers and Browns.

Following his NFL career, Heiden was able to stay in the league as a coach. He was hired in 2013 by good friend and former Browns offensive coordinator Bruce Arians.

Arians was hired as the Cardinals' head coach prior to the 2013 season, and Heiden joined him as assistant special teams/assistant tight ends coach.

"You get a job with Bruce and you just shut your mouth and play hard, just like when you were a player," Heiden said.

The Cardinals seem destined to finally get Heiden to a Super Bowl, as one of the up-and-coming teams in the NFL.

In 2015, they were one game away from the Super Bowl, falling in the NFC Championship Game to the Carolina Panthers.

With the knowledge base of Heiden helping the Cardinals now as a coach, there's no doubt that Arizona is a better team and ready for bigger and better things.

As a player, Heiden will always remember his time in Cleveland, and the fans that made his eight seasons special.

CHAPTER 8

DAVID GRAYSON

Linebacker 1987–1990
The Game: September 10, 1989, vs Pittsburgh Steelers at Three
Rivers Stadium
CLEVELAND BROWNS 51—PITTSBURGH STEELERS 0

FORMER CLEVELAND BROWNS linebacker David Grayson was born into a football family and took a page from his father's book, making it to the NFL for four seasons with the Browns from 1987 to 1990.

Born in San Diego, California, Grayson played his high school ball at Lincoln High in Southeast San Diego, a school that also produced such NFL players as Hall of Fame running back Marcus Allen and former Denver Broncos running back Terrell Davis, as well as his own father, Dave Grayson.

His father played in the AFL for three years, playing with the Dallas Texans, Kansas City Chiefs, and Oakland Raiders, and then went on to six years in the NFL.

Grayson Senior was an All-Pro defensive back from Lincoln High and even played in Super Bowl II with the Oakland Raiders in a loss to the Green Bay Packers.

His son played his college ball at Fresno State and then moved on to the NFL Draft, being a pick of the San Francisco 49ers in the 1987 NFL Draft. The 49ers, however, later released him, and he was picked up by the Browns.

Notes on David Grayson

Years Played: 1987-1990
Position: Linebacker
Height: 6'2"
Weight: 230
Hometown: San Diego, CA
Current Residence: Encinitas, CA
Occupation: Works in the Finance Industry
Accomplishments: Born and raised in San Diego, CA, and played his high school ball at Abraham Lincoln High School. Attended Fresno State, where he played for the Bulldogs before he was drafted in the eighth round of the 1987 Draft, 217th overall, by the San Francisco 49ers. He was cut by the 49ers, and the Browns brought him into play during the strike season of 1987. Started five games his rookie season and from there stuck as a member of the defense for four seasons. During that time started 37 of 53 games, intercepting three passes, recovering four fumbles, and scoring three times to go along with eight sacks. Was the AFC Defensive Player of the Week for week one of the 1989 season, as he scored twice in a 51–0 win over the Pittsburgh Steelers at Three Rivers Stadium. His father, Dave, played in the AFL and also the NFL, and appeared in Super Bowl II as a member of the Oakland Raiders during a 33–14 loss to the Green Bay Packers.
Nickname: None

David Grayson sacks the Bills' Jim Kelly. (AP Photo)

"I got drafted by the Niners in the eighth round in '87, and I remember Ronnie Lott telling Bill Walsh at the time, 'You're making a mistake, the kid can play,'" Grayson said.

"Later that year we went to San Francisco to play them, and I had a fumble return for a touchdown, and Walsh said on national TV that I was the biggest mistake he had ever made as far as releasing a player."

Grayson, unlike his dad in Super Bowl II, never got to play in the big game, but got close, playing with the Browns in 1987 as the team lost the AFC Championship in the game forever known as "The Fumble."

How he wound up in Cleveland is a whole other story, joining the team during the 1987 player strike, and sticking with them for four seasons.

"I was a California kid, so Cleveland was the farthest East I had ever lived. I got drafted by the 49ers and got released, and came to Cleveland during the strike in 1987," Grayson said. "I was kind of a deer in the headlights. I didn't know what to expect."

What he got was a very well-established football team, coming off a season in which they went 12–4 and lost the AFC Championship Game to the Denver Broncos in overtime at home.

They also had a great group of players on both sides of the ball, as well as a great coach in Marty Schottenheimer, who was a master motivator as well as a coach who was able to get the most out of his players.

"Once I got there I was pleasantly surprised. Marty was a great coach, he was extremely honest; we probably worked harder than any team in the league at that point," Grayson said. "Dave Adolph was my linebackers coach, probably one of the best coaches I played under.

"It was a great time, we were winning, the Browns were coming off 'The Drive,' but they were a winning team, and a great group of guys, very funny bunch of characters.

"The biggest two were Frank Minnifield and Hanford Dixon. We would stretch and those guys would be cracking jokes, it just lightened up everything."

The 1987 Browns were on a mission, a team that felt they had been robbed of a shot at the Super Bowl the year before, and they went 10–5, winning six of their last eight games, good enough to win the AFC Central.

A highlight of that team was the play of their two corners, Dixon and Minnifield, known as the two players who founded the famous "Dawg Pound," something that is still very popular with Browns fans.

"As far as their play, it was amazing at that time," Grayson recalls of the two corners.

"To have two corners that you could just put man-on-man the whole game, it was a luxury, and those guys had no problems with it either."

The 1987 season ended with that fateful fumble in Denver, but for Grayson it was just the start of a solid four-year stint in Cleveland.

He started five games at the right outside linebacker spot that first season and then in 1988 moved to the left side at outside linebacker, starting 14 games and registering five sacks.

Grayson wasn't sure just how much playing time he would get as the team went out and shored up their linebacker core in the draft following the 1987 campaign.

"I was a player they brought in, made the team, and I started five games my rookie year, and I thought I was done when they drafted Van Waters and Clifford Charlton, two linebackers, and when it came to training camp I just beat both of them out," Grayson said.

By the end of the 1988 season, Grayson was a mainstay on the Browns defense, and it also was the dawn of a new era in Browns football, as Bud Carson moved in to take over for Schottenheimer, who left the team just days after a Christmas Eve wild-card game loss at home to the Houston Oilers.

Grayson was used to Carson and vice versa, so when the decision was made to make Bud the head coach, it was something that Grayson was all for.

"We really liked Bud a lot; he was a player's coach," Grayson says. "I remember one game, it was one of our first games, might have been a preseason game; it was at the stadium, and our defense had meetings upstairs, and the offense downstairs.

"Bud comes upstairs and basically changes our whole defense. He was really smart when it came to football, a real mastermind. He sometimes got a little carried away, and just changed everything.

"It was, basically, the first year our defense was ranked pretty high, and we were all over the place, and then the next year, once we figured out what we were doing, we were horrible. We went 3–13."

That was year two under Carson, and while that season was one of disaster, no one could have imagined how the 1989 season would start.

The team opened the season with a road game against their biggest rivals, the Pittsburgh Steelers, and it was a game that turned out to be the best of Grayson's career.

The Game

The game I recall where I played really well, against all odds, was when we played Pittsburgh, in Pittsburgh, in the opener of the 1989 season.

I had a bad neck, and we beat them bad, 51–0. I got AFC Defensive Player of the Week that game. I scored a pair of touchdowns.

It was Bud Carson's first game as our coach, and we were fine with him coming in; we knew what we could do, and if you think about it, the core of our defense didn't change for a couple years.

We had Hanford Dixon, Frank Minnifield, Mike Johnson, Clay Matthews, and then on offense we had Kevin Mack, Earnest Byner, and then our offensive line was intact.

Thinking about it, we had a team that was pretty intact during my career there. Compare to now where a team does well, and they get broken up after that; I hate to see that.

Going in to play Pittsburgh, you better expect a dogfight, regardless of the records or anything. You might walk in, but you are for sure going to limp out of that game.

We expected a normal, typical hard Pittsburgh game. We just got some breaks, and things were falling apart for them. I made a couple of plays, the two touchdowns, that didn't help them.

It was one of those games where it snowballed, and it was like, "Please run the clock and put them out of their misery."

The first touchdown I scored I basically stole the ball away from Louis Lipps; they were running a reverse, and I didn't fall for it.

When he came over to my side, I thought he was going to try and juke me, or run around me, but he came toward me and I felt the ball and just started tugging, and it came loose, and I thought they were going to blow the whistle.

I ran into the end zone, and everyone was cheering, and I saw my teammates running toward me, and I just sort of dropped the ball and ran for the sidelines, because I knew we had to go back out on the field again.

At the time that put us up, 17–0, and we were just off and running.

The second score I had they were throwing a pass, and their quarterback Bubby Brister threw it, and it went off the fingers of their fullback, Merril Hoge.

I caught it and I thought as I was running, "You've got to be kidding me." It just fell into my hands and it wasn't a sharp tip, it just kind of floated. I thought, "I can get used to this."

By then it got us up, 44–0, and it was just kind of like a dream, looking at the scoreboard playing in a game like that.

We were waiting for them to come back, or to start playing better. Even after we got up big, we just were waiting for them to push back, and then time ran out.

That's one of those days where you as a defensive coordinator, you dream of. Holding a team to five first downs and 53 total yards, it doesn't get much better than that.

Of course, coaches can always find negative plays and notwhat, or plays you make a mistake on, and that's never fun.

Film session I had more butterflies than going into any game. It can be brutal. More so if you're a guy that tries to make excuses. The coaches don't want to hear any of that.

That day not much went wrong for us. Our offense had the ball over 40 minutes, and frankly I don't even recall how we were on the field for just 17 minutes.

I remember we collected a lot of turnovers, eight of them in all.

After a while, I think it just snowballs to the other team, and people just start making mistakes. It was a fun day.

The Aftermath

The year 1989 was another successful one for the Browns, as the team reached the postseason yet again, going 9–6–1 and winning the AFC Central.

The team defeated the Buffalo Bills at home in an exciting AFC Divisional Playoff game and traveled to Denver yet again with a trip to the Super Bowl on the line.

Unlike the first two AFC Title Games against the Broncos, this time they were outplayed basically from start to finish, losing, 37–21, ending another season one game short of the biggest game in the NFL.

After '89, the team fell apart quickly, and while they started the season with another win over the Steelers, the club only won one more game by the time they reached their bye week in week 10, sitting at 2–7.

Carson was canned after a 42–0 home loss to the Bills, and Jim Shofner came on as interim head coach for the final seven games, and the team limped to a woeful 3–13 season.

In his final season with the Browns, Grayson once again was a mainstay on defense, playing in all 16 games, starting eight, and collecting one interception and one fumble recovery.

He moved on to his hometown team in San Diego on the Chargers and played in just one game there before leaving the NFL for good after the 1991 season.

Grayson moved for good back to Encinitas, California, after spending a few years in Oklahoma, working in and out of the finance industry while taking care of his family.

He always recalls his days in Cleveland, a time very different and very much appreciated over the lifestyle he had living in California.

"Cleveland as a city, culturewise, was more dynamic than, say, San Diego," Grayson said.

"San Diego is a more conservative city, while Cleveland was more passionate, especially about their football. People here just wanted to shake your hand, and that was really cool.

"It was nice to have that change of pace."

CHAPTER 9

BRIAN KINCHEN

Tight End 1991–1995
The Game: November 26, 1995, vs Pittsburgh Steelers at
Cleveland Stadium
PITTSBURGH STEELERS 20—CLEVELAND BROWNS 17

WHEN BRIAN KINCHEN was named the Cleveland Browns starting tight end prior to the 1993 campaign, he thought it was a dream come true.

Little did he know the utter torture that awaited him and his teammates two seasons later, as the team went through one of the most difficult seasons in NFL history.

The year was 1995, and the Browns were coming off an 11–5 season in 1994 in which the team seemed to be on the upswing. They had reached the playoffs and had even beaten the New England Patriots in a wild card game at Cleveland Stadium.

Then, in one fell swoop, owner Art Modell turned the team and its fans upside down by announcing the team would move to Baltimore following that season.

Kinchen, who had waited his whole life to be a starter in the NFL, felt firsthand the bitterness the fans were feeling, not only toward Modell, but also how they seemed to turn on the Browns players as a whole.

The story of Kinchen started with his dad, Gaynell "Gus" Kinchen, who was a member of the National Champion LSU Tigers football team in 1958.

Notes on Brian Kinchen

Years Played: 1991–1995
Position: Tight End
Height: 6'2"
Weight: 240
Hometown: Baton Rouge, LA
Current Residence: Baton Rouge, LA
Occupation: Runs a Football Camp in Baton Rouge
Accomplishments: Played his college ball at LSU, pulling in 48 passes for 523 yards and six touchdowns in three seasons. Was taken in the 12th round of the 1988 draft by the Miami Dolphins, 320th pick overall. Played under Hall of Fame coach Don Shula for three years in Miami, where in 36 games, no starts, caught just two passes for 15 yards. In Cleveland with the Browns played five years, making 38 starts while playing in 75 games. Pulled in 73 catches for 795 yards and three touchdowns. Had his best year the following season after the Browns moved to Baltimore, where he started 16 games, pulling in 55 catches for 581 yards and one score. In his career had 160 catches for 1,648 yards and seven touchdowns. Was the long snapper on the Patriots' Super Bowl winning team in the 2003 season, snapping back for the game-winning field goal on the final play of the game. Brother Todd also played in the NFL. Spent some time post-football career as a commentator on ESPN U.
Nickname: None

Browns tight end Brian Kinchen runs a pass route during a game. (Photo courtesy of Brian Kinchen)

Brian was born in Baton Rouge, Louisiana, and followed in the footsteps of his dad, playing his college ball at LSU.

It was there, as a tight end, that he rounded into form, but he was just as valuable as a long snapper, getting the ball to the holder on field goals, and to the punter on punts.

He was drafted by legendary coach Don Shula and the Miami Dolphins in the 12th round of the 1988 NFL Draft, the 320th pick.

Shula felt that the best thing for Kinchen would be to compete as a special teams player and continue to long snap, and his plays at tight end in Miami were few and far between.

"I had always wanted to be a starter in the NFL, and be a significant factor," Kinchen recalls.

"I was in Miami for three years, and Don Shula wouldn't let me do anything but play special teams and be a backup."

Kinchen wound up with the Browns prior to the 1991 season but still had problems getting into the game as a tight end.

"When I got to Cleveland Bill Belichick didn't let me get on the field as a tight end. His logic was, I was too valuable as a long snapper to risk getting injured," Kinchen said.

The chance for Kinchen to make it as a starter almost never came. In his first game he was called upon to long snap, and it was a nerve-racking experience with a roster spot on the line.

"My first game in Cleveland was a pretty traumatic game. I came in as a long snapper, because two of the other long snappers on the team had gotten hurt," Kinchen said.

"I came in, and we were playing the Cincinnati Bengals, and I remember we had a field goal situation at the end of the first half.

"I threw a low snap; it wasn't a bad snap, but the holder had to trap it. The holder was Brian Hansen, and he was a really good holder, but he didn't handle it really well, and he didn't get it up correctly.

"It looked terrible, and obviously it was the fault of the new long snapper, which was me, since I threw a low ball."

The nip and tuck affair at Cleveland Stadium saw the Browns leading the Bengals, 11–3, entering the fourth quarter, but all Kinchen could think about was that low snap earlier in the game.

"The whole rest of the game I'm on the sideline and I'm just thinking, 'I'm going to get released like the guy did in week one because of this bad snap.'" Kinchen said.

The Bengals scored ten points in the fourth quarter to take a 13–11 lead, but the Browns on their final drive drove downfield for a chance at a game-winner by Stover.

"We ended up kicking a 45-yard field goal with eight seconds on the clock in the open end of Cleveland Stadium, and Matt Stover, who was in his first season, came on and he had never kicked a game winner in his life.

"It wasn't a doubt, we were down, 13–11, and if he doesn't make the kick we lose the game. I pretty much knew in my mind if Matt didn't make the kick I was probably done.

"Well, Matt nailed the kick, I keep my job, and two years later I finally achieve that goal of finally becoming a starter in the NFL," Kinchen said.

Kinchen remained as the long snapper on the Browns roster and continued to work hard. Finally, before the 1993 season, he showed enough to grab the starting position for the Browns at the tight end spot.

"For me, my third year when they named me the starter was pretty monumental; it was kind of the stamp of validation that I was worthy, to be one of 30 guys in the NFL to be starting on that team as a tight end, it was pretty significant for me," Kinchen remembers.

In 1993, Kinchen caught 29 passes for 347 yards and two scores, and the next season pulled in 24 passes for 234 yards and a score.

The 1995 season, though, it all crumbled for the Browns. Modell announced the team was leaving the city at the conclusion of the year, and a season that held so much promise fell apart from there.

The team, following that official announcement, still had three more home games to play, with one on November 26 at home against the rival Pittsburgh Steelers, who had beaten the Browns three times in 1994.

The Game

One game that I really remember well was that last year, 1995, when (Browns owner Art) Modell had either intentionally or unintentionally leaked that we were leaving.

We had a really good start to that year, we started out 3–1, but then after the move announcement came down, I remember well that Pittsburgh game at home.

I remember us getting booed on the field, and people cheering for the Pittsburgh Steelers in our stadium. It was just so surreal sitting there as a player.

We knew the fans weren't necessarily booing us, they were booing Modell, that was the reason for it; but at the same time, we were the representation of the Browns on the field at the time.

I tell the story so often. I mean, I know we are NFL players on a team, and it's not any significance in life whatsoever; it's not life or death or war or civil unrest.

But for us, it was our occupation at the time, and it really made us feel like a bunch of worthless players who had no home, and like no one cared whether we won or lost.

Granted, probably not everyone felt that way, but given my nature, I had a very insecure nature, a very unworthy nature about me, and I just stood in that stadium in disbelief.

I wondered how people could be this cruel, and how could the fans not understand what it does to us, and how it makes us feel, and how could this happen in our own stadium.

I remember the first time I heard it, and I just had to look around and I wondered if this was really happening.

I was always really impressed with the Cleveland fans, and Browns fans. I remember being out in Los Angeles for a game and hordes of Browns fans surrounding our bus and thinking, "How is this possible?"

I never grasped the concept of that fan base and how great it was, but obviously in that moment of that Pittsburgh game it was very different.

I remember it so vividly because Pittsburgh was the team we disliked the most, and they were really our rival in a sense.

You just stood there and wondered, "How is this happening, how is this possible?"

They were the team I had such little success against, I think I was like 2–19 against them in my career. So for me on that day it was almost devastating in a sense that this great fan base could turn on its own team like that.

You fast-forward to our last home game that season, the last game in Cleveland Stadium, and the players were running up to the fans, taking pictures and stuff, and people were taking chairs out of the stadium.

I just sat back kind of neutral because of that whole moment against Pittsburgh. I felt like we were kind of shunned by everybody, and I felt like "you basically dumped on us when you found out this was happening, and now you want to be all nostalgic about it."

No NFL player will probably ever feel those types of emotions on an NFL field ever again. It was just the most bizarre year.

I've said it before, I wouldn't wish it on my worst enemy to have to endure something like that. You're living a dream by playing in the NFL, but it was like you were a team and a player that no one cared about.

I guess in a sense I probably blame Modell for it; at the same time I understood it. The day you walk in the NFL is the day you understand it's a business. It's not the game you played in college, and it won't be ever again.

I always wanted to really know why he had to do it that way, why couldn't he figure the whole thing out and just keep it under wraps.

It was just a very bittersweet ending to that time in Cleveland.

The Aftermath

The game that late November afternoon in Cleveland was secondary to the way the fans responded to the hometown Browns, but in the end the Steelers were three points better than the Browns, pulling out a 20–17 win.

The Browns' season ended with the team going 5–11. They won just two games after their 3–1 start, and one game after Modell announced the team was moving—their final home game at Cleveland Stadium against the Cincinnati Bengals.

It was as painful a season a city and its fans could experience, but what made it downright numbing was the fact the team was leaving Cleveland behind.

"I am reluctant to talk about that because I don't think it comes across that well to the Cleveland fans, but it was just the most bizarre existence for an NFL team or a player to ever have," Kinchen said.

"You're doing something you always dreamed of doing, but you never could imagine you would feel so unappreciated."

The 1995 season was one that was stressful on the Browns' front office, the players, and coaching staff. Everyone involved felt the pressure of trying to do well on Sunday, yet during the week it was nothing but chatter about Modell and the team leaving the city behind.

"I just remember those games and being miserable, going out there and doing your best, and no one really seems to care," Kinchen said.

"When the rumors started to come out, no one knew if it was real. Then, when it became real, it just seemed like everyone walked around in a cloud.

"I remember Art standing in front of a team meeting and speaking, and how he said he guaranteed that Bill Belichick would be the coach when he moved to Baltimore the following year.

"It was just a flat-out lie to try and stabilize us, and try to rally us. He tried to play it off like it would be business as usual, but in Baltimore."

Kinchen made the move with the team to Baltimore, where he played three seasons, from 1996 to 1998. He had his best season in 1996, when starting 16 games. He caught 55 passes for 581 yards and a score for Baltimore.

His story took an amazing twist after he walked away from the game following his release from the Carolina Panthers in 2000.

Three years later, Kinchen was teaching Bible Studies class to seventh graders, and was also a middle school coach and volunteer at LSU with Nick Saban, far away from his days in the NFL.

That's when the phone rang, and on the other line were the New England Patriots, and despite its being week 15 of the 2003 NFL season, they wanted Kinchen to return to be their long snapper for their Super Bowl run.

The 41-year-old came back and delivered a perfect snap in Super Bowl XXXVIII on the final play as Patriots kicker Adam Vinatieri kicked a field goal to win the game, earning Kinchen a ring.

It was the ultimate comeback story, and one that put Kinchen in the spotlight, from a player who felt he was going to be let go after a shaky snap in his first game in Cleveland in 1991 to snapping for the game-winning kick in the biggest game of his life.

"Long snapping was the key to getting me in the league in Miami, and, obviously, while in Cleveland it helped me stay in the league and gave me the opportunity to fulfill my ultimate dream, which was to get that validation and that sense of self-worth," Kinchen said.

"I've always had self-doubt issues, and football was my outlet."

CHAPTER 10

HERMAN FONTENOT

Running Back 1985–1988
The Game: December 21, 1986, vs San Diego Chargers at
Cleveland Stadium
CLEVELAND BROWNS 47—SAN DIEGO CHARGERS 17

GROWING UP IN St. Elizabeth, Texas, former Cleveland Browns running back Herman Fontenot never dreamed about playing alongside some of the greats in the National Football League.

He played football for the love of it, and even after his four seasons at LSU, from 1981 to 1984, Fontenot thought that his playing days on the gridiron were over after he didn't get selected that year in the NFL Draft.

"When I wasn't drafted back then they would send you letters to come out and try out, which was exciting to see the different letters from different teams," Fontenot said. "I had a stack of letters, but I chose the Cleveland Browns because I had a couple LSU guys that were going to go there and try out.

"Not really knowing the process, that's how I got to Cleveland. Unbeknown to me, though, there was a letter, in my bedroom, and I didn't see it, from the Pittsburgh Steelers. Needless to say, I was like, 'Wow,' but I went with the group of guys I knew to Cleveland."

The opportunity for Fontenot parlayed into a productive six-year NFL career, playing four for the Browns and two more for the Green Bay Packers.

While he was confident he could play in the NFL when he made the Browns roster, he felt that his playing days at LSU were the catapult

Notes on Herman Fontenot

Years Played: 1985–1990
Position: Running Back
Height: 6'0"
Weight: 206
Hometown: St.Elizabeth, Texas
Current Residence: Houston, Texas
Occupation: Works for a company called 3D Print Bureau of Texas
Accomplishments: Played six seasons in the NFL, four with the Browns and two with the Packers. Was undrafted out of LSU but made the Browns roster in 1985. In six NFL seasons was more of a pass catcher than a runner, catching 143 passes for 1,453 yards and six touchdowns. Ran 102 yards for 370 yards and two scores. Is the only Browns player in history to catch touchdowns in back-to-back playoff games, which he did in 1986 against the New York Jets and Denver Broncos. In the two playoff games in 1986, caught 12 passes for 128 yards and two scores.
Nickname: None

to being ready to go at it every Sunday for 60 minutes with the best the NFL had to offer.

"The hardest part about football in my life was in college. That was the roughest, the toughest, and the most challenging to me," Fontenot said.

"By the time I left LSU and went to the Cleveland Browns, competing against those guys, it wasn't difficult.

"At that time we had created the Dawg Pound, our defense, which at the time was one of the best in the NFL. So those were the guys that I was competing against.

"Those guys had made a name for themselves. Chip Banks, Clay Matthews, Handford Dixon, Frank Minnifield . . . you can go on and on and on.

"Competing against those guys daily made me think that I could compete in the NFL."

It was not only going up against a very good defense. Fontenot was part of a developing offense under quarterback Bernie Kosar that would eventually lead the team to two AFC Championship Games in 1986 and 1987.

Those seasons were two of the most memorable in Browns history. The fan base was as strong as it had ever been, and players on the Browns were treated on the streets of Cleveland like celebrities.

"We had a chance to develop a relationship with the fans because we were winning. We were in certain places at certain times with a smile on our face, with our head up instead of down because we hadn't lost games again and again," Fontenot said.

"We did put our heads down on the outcome of big games: 'The Drive' and the 'The Fumble.' We had some difficult times for some of the younger fellas like myself. We had some great teams, it was sad they had to be broken up.

"The time I remember in the Cleveland area was incredible.

"We had the Flats, Shooters was just created, we were young men, and we were high profile playing in AFC Championship games, it was great. A lot of great relationships were made, and personal relationships, inside and outside of football."

Fontenot's best season came in 1986 with a Browns team on the cusp of a Super Bowl berth. Playing alongside both Kevin Mack and Ernest Byner, Fontenot caught 47 passes for 559 yards and a touchdown, rushing for 105 yards and a score.

His biggest game of the season came in the regular season finale, as the Browns were preparing for a playoff run with the number one seed. The team hosted a 4–11 San Diego Chargers team on the Lakefront four days before Christmas.

The Game

My personal game goes back to 1986, and it was the last regular season game for us, and it was a game in which I threw a touchdown and ran a touchdown, something pretty remarkable for not being drafted to even play in the NFL.

Here, two years after, I was running and catching and throwing touchdowns in the NFL; it was all exciting to me.

I also saw a stat where I am the only player in Cleveland Browns history to score a touchdown in two consecutive playoff games, which I did that season against the Jets and Broncos.

Things like that someone always had to bring to my attention because I don't know a thing about the Browns history, but it is pretty cool.

I remember the weather that day as being sunshine and beautiful. The sun was shining, it was a little cold, but that day was a beautiful day for that time of year, which was surprising.

It was as if the skies lit up, and everything we wanted to do we accomplished.

As far as the throw, it came in the first quarter, and it was a 46-yard touchdown throw to Webster Slaughter. We always would practice it every week.

I was out there throwing, and I was able to throw it 60, 70 yards.

For him to be open at that time, it wasn't a surprise. Webster was one of the greatest wide receivers to me of all time.

My favorite sport was baseball, and that helped me as we practiced throwing, and we practiced the play every week.

I had a calmness when I was on the field, and the ability I had to focus and be calm about it, it was just natural, just like in practice, we practiced like we played.

We went out and we would practice hard, so when we went out on Sunday we played like we practiced. When you practice a certain way and then a play works, I was not surprised when Webster was open on the play, which gave us the lead and started us on our way.

It was just second nature, something I had been doing for quite some time, something I did in high school, and it was something the coaches caught on to.

I would go out before practice and throw the ball to receivers. I would actually warm up for the game by throwing long balls to Frank Minnifield; that was his pregame warm up.

There was no arrogance about it for me; it was just special as a young man to have the opportunity to play among the best football players of all time.

I ran for a score in the third quarter that put us up, 34–10, and it felt great. We were on our way to a big win, and we were moving on to our first playoff game, and we were just jacked; it was great being a part of that team.

The energy in the stadium, I just absolutely loved the Cleveland Browns fans. They were and still are special.

The Aftermath

The Browns were in their prime. Kosar and the offense put up 24.4 points per game, good for fifth in the NFL that season.

The defense was ranked 11th, with young stars like the two corners, Minnefield and Dixon, who founded the "Dawg Pound," a beloved part of Cleveland Browns football to this day.

The Browns were able to win one of the most memorable games in NFL history in their first playoff game, lasting out a double-overtime game against the New York Jets, 23–20.

They led the AFC Title Game, 20–13, with fewer than six minutes to go, but were the victims of one of the most gut-wrenching losses in history when Denver Broncos quarterback John Elway led Denver on what is still referred to this day as "The Drive."

The following season, Denver once again bounced the Browns out of the playoffs in the AFC Title Game, one that is still recalled to this day with a Byner misplay known simply as "The Fumble."

Fontenot played for the Browns through the 1988 season, lasting as long as head coach Marty Schottenheimer, then landed with the Green Bay Packers.

The running back spent two seasons with the Packers, catching 71 passes for four touchdowns in two seasons with Green Bay.

The end for Fontenot came quickly, as, one day following the 1991 season, he simply decided his NFL career was over at the age of 27.

"I just never got all that jacked about football, and one day I just decided I didn't want to play anymore. That's why I didn't keep playing with Green Bay," Fontenot said.

"Being a part of the Cleveland Browns there was such a bond, and I just couldn't find that excitement anymore."

Twenty-five years later, Fontenot fights another battle, a very different one off the field.

He is part of a company called 3D Print Bureau of Texas, a firm that specializes in 3D printing of model hearts for doctors and hospitals.

"This is the most exciting point in my life, believe it or not," Fontenot notes.

"I actually take CT scans of patients' hearts, and from that we are able to build a 3D print of that person's heart, which will give a doctor a chance to see what may be wrong with that person's heart."

While he's enjoying his life in Houston, he still fondly recalls his days with the Browns and even pays a visit to Browns fans now and then.

"One of the things I do when I go to different cities is I go online, and when I move to places like Clearwater, Florida, and Tampa I would go online and contact Cleveland Browns backers, and I would show up and surprise them," Fontenot said.

"Talk about some incredible fans, they were so surprised, and this is well after I played. I'm talking about seven years ago I started doing it. Now I'm living in Houston, and I've yet to embark upon the Houston Browns backers, but I will. I think we have the best in all of sports."

CHAPTER 11

TOM TUPA

Punter 1993–1995
The Game: September 4, 1994, vs Cincinnati Bengals at Riverfront Stadium
CLEVELAND BROWNS 28—CINCINNATI BENGALS 20

TOM TUPA TRULY was a homegrown player, who for two seasons got to live out his dream playing for his hometown team.

For the 1994 and 1995 seasons, Tupa was the Browns punter, being thrust into a role that he was first told he was not good enough to handle in the NFL.

Tupa was born in 1966 in Cleveland and played his high school ball at local Brecksville-Broadview Heights High School, where he excelled at football, basketball, and baseball.

While he enjoyed playing quarterback, he also enjoyed punting, which is something that came naturally to him.

"I punted since I was little, I went through all the youth leagues, middle school, all that stuff punting," Tupa said.

"I did all the 'Punt, Pass and Kick' competitions when I was little, and I punted in high school, as well.

"For some reason punting came natural to me. In high school I punted well and became an All-American in high school punting.

"I started to get looks from schools, first for punting, and then also for playing quarterback."

Tupa's college career saw him stay in state, going two hours away to Columbus to play for the Ohio State Buckeyes, where he was a standout punter, earning All-American honors as a senior.

Notes on Tom Tupa

Years Played: 1988–2004
Position: Punter/Quarterback
Height: 6'4"
Weight: 225
Hometown: Cleveland, OH
Current Residence: Brecksville, OH
Occupation: Athletic Director at Brecksville-Broadview Hts. High School
Accomplishments: Was a winner in the annual NFL Punt, Pass and Kick competition and was a semi-finalist three times. Led the Brecksville-Broadview Heights Bees to a state title in basketball while in high school, putting up 20.8 points per game. Was a *USA Today* All-American. Also played quarterback while in high school. Sat for three years at Ohio State before finally starting his senior season. That year he threw for 15 touchdowns and 12 interceptions and 2,252 yards. He was a four-time football letterman at Ohio State and played in the Hula Bowl All-Star game his senior season in 1988. Played for seven different teams in his NFL career, is part of the New England Patriots All-1990s Team. Was a part of their team that went to Super Bowl XXXI, falling to the Green Bay Packers. Won a Super Bowl as part of the Tampa Bay Buccaneers in the 2002 season, winning Super Bowl XXXVII.
Nickname: "Two-Point"

He also had significant time under center. In his senior year at Ohio State he was also the Buckeyes' starting quarterback.

In that 1987 season at Ohio State, Tupa threw for 2,252 yards, 15 touchdowns, and 12 interceptions.

Upon entering the NFL Draft in 1988, he was selected by the Phoenix Cardinals, who took him in the third round with the 68th overall pick.

He was drafted as both a quarterback and punter but was given the news early in his NFL days that he wouldn't be punting anymore.

"I go out to Phoenix and work with the special teams coach the first mini-camp, and he basically said, 'Watch me punt.' He never really felt I would ever be able to punt in the league," Tupa said.

"He told me that straight out."

In three seasons with the Cardinals, he punted just six times, all in the 1989 season. He did start 13 games at quarterback for the Cardinals in his three years there, going 4–9 in those starts.

Overall, he threw for just over 3,000 yards in his career with Phoenix, throwing nine touchdowns and 22 interceptions.

He moved on to the Indianapolis Colts for one season in 1992, then halfway through the 1993 season got a call from his hometown Cleveland team under rather tough circumstances.

"When I first came here it was kind of a strange situation, because when they cut Bernie Kosar, that's when I came in," Tupa said.

"That was kind of a strange situation because I knew Bernie. I was out on the street at the time. I came in for a few games in 1993; I was only in for a brief period.

"I didn't even touch the field. I was the emergency quarterback, so it wasn't like I was replacing Bernie, but knowing the following the Browns had during my childhood and college when they were at the forefront of the NFL, it was strange coming in during that situation.

"There was so much talk about him leaving the club and Belichick that, honestly, I was pretty much under the radar, which was a good thing for me."

Tupa was back out of the NFL after the 1993 season when special teams coach Scott O'Brien called him, asking him if he had interest in coming back to the Browns as a punter.

"Obviously, I said, 'Yes,' and things went well in the offseason, and that's when I really started my punting career," Tupa recalls.

Tupa's "second" career in the NFL took off: in 1994, he punted 80 times, averaging 40.1 yards per kick, with a 60-yard punt during the season, to boot.

While he was a solid punter, that's not what Tupa is exactly known for.

The 1994 season in the NFL was the first in which the league adopted the two-point conversion, a rule that had been in the AFL from 1960 to 1969, but never in the NFL.

Opening day 1994 was the first time any team in the NFL could go for two points instead of the standard one-point extra point.

Then Browns coach Bill Belichick knew exactly at what point to pull the trigger on the new rule: the first score for the Browns on opening day.

Tupa would have never guessed that he would become a big part of the new rule, and that he would forever earn a new nickname: "Two-Point Tupa."

The Game

That first game coming back in 1994 we played down in Cincinnati against the Bengals. I just happened to be at the right place at the right time.

No one really before that had to work on stopping a two-point play, so it was a wide-open play since no one really knew how to prepare to stop it.

It was a play that Scott O'Brien drew up, and really it was a no-brainer for me. All I had to do when I took the snap was not trip and I was okay.

You know how Belichick is, he goes over every situation you could probably think of. So when the game comes around, you have at least practiced it and are aware of what to do.

We practiced the two-point plays all throughout camp and had all kinds of plays, those things are always practiced with him. You're always prepared with coach Belichick.

We had decided already we were going to go for two on the first touchdown. We knew from scouting the kind of look we were going to get, so it was just a called play, and it was the exact look that we had thought they were going to show us.

I just had to pick the ball up and run over the left side.

The funny thing is, talking about it being the first game of the season and everything, someone told me that I scored the first two-point conversion just before anyone else on any other team had scored one.

There was one scored just a little bit after me, which is kind of funny because, as they say, timing is everything, and I was able to score the first two-point conversion before anyone on that same day to start the 1994 season.

When I scored the first two-point conversion I really wasn't thinking, "Wow, I just scored the first NFL two-point conversion," or anything like that. We were just kind of celebrating on our first try on our first game we were able to put it in for two points.

I don't think anyone really realized till after the game that the particular one we scored on the first drive, that it was the first one scored in the NFL.

We scored a few of those two-point conversions that year. Scott O'Brien, he was just an unbelievable special teams coach.

We had practiced different scenarios. Fortunately, we were able to either run it or pitch it, or even throw it in, out of that kicking formation.

We practiced a bunch of them, and overall we got pretty good at them; we scored four that season.

I got the nickname "Two-Point Tupa" after I scored three of the two-point conversions, and I was fortunate to be in that situation, and more so to be able to make that first one.

The name to me is kind of nice; it's nice that people recognize the name with NFL history.

The Aftermath

The 1994 Browns were one of the surprises of the NFL that season, going from 7–9 in 1993 to winning 11 games.

The problem with the '94 team is they were in a division with the equally good Pittsburgh Steelers, who beat the Browns twice during the regular season and ended the year 12–4, the number one seed in the AFC.

The Browns played their final playoff game in the history of Cleveland Municipal Stadium on New Year's Day, 1995, beating Hall of Fame coach Bill Parcells and the New England Patriots, 20–13.

Six days later, the team went into Three Rivers Stadium to play the Steelers, and, unlike the first two times they played, this time it wasn't even close.

The Steelers put up 24 points against the usually stout Browns defense in the first half, led it 24–3 at halftime, and took home a 29–9 win to end the Browns' season.

The following season, Tupa was once again the Browns' punter, and the team got off to a good start, going 3–1 after a home win over the Kansas City Chiefs.

The Browns were picked by a number of "experts" to be the team to beat in the AFC, and the city was riding high thinking there was a very good chance the team would make its first Super Bowl.

Little did they know that a disaster no one could have seen coming awaited the team and its fans.

Rumors started to rumble in late October that then owner Art Modell was in talks with the city of Baltimore to move the Browns, a step that would devastate the city and the team's 1995 season.

The move was made official following a bad home loss to the Houston Oilers that dropped the record to 4–5, and basically the season was over the next day when Modell stood on a platform in Baltimore and announced the Browns were moving.

"That 1994 team, we had so much talent on the team and things were going in the right direction; then in 1995 we were okay at the start of the season, then once things got out that we were moving things just started to snowball," Tupa remembers.

The team went into a complete tailspin, going 1–6 over the last seven weeks as the city and fans dealt with the harsh reality that there would no longer be football in Cleveland.

The final game in Cleveland was the final win for the team, as they closed out Cleveland Municipal Stadium on December 17, 1995, with a 26–10 win over the Bengals.

"It was a strange situation knowing that the team was leaving; there were no advertisements in the stadium, there were people protesting, things really fell apart after word got out," Tupa said.

Tupa would go on to bigger and better. His career continued as a punter in the NFL. He reached the Pro Bowl as a punter with the New York Jets in 1999, averaging 45.2 yards per kick that season.

He reached the pinnacle of his NFL career in 2002 when he kicked for the Tampa Bay Buccaneers, who went 12–4 and defeated the Oakland Raiders in the Super Bowl, earning a ring for the kid from Cleveland.

Tupa left the game after the 2004 season, and while he returned home to Brecksville to watch his sons play football at his high school alma mater while serving as the athletic director for the school, he recalls with fondness those two seasons with the Browns, despite the outcome in '95.

"As I think back about the players we had, that roster, we were kind of set up. Defensively, offensively, Vinny at quarterback, Steve Everett at center, Orlando Brown on that line, he was one of the bigger human beings you'll ever see.

"We were headed in the right direction, we had everything, all phases of the game. Things were great until news got out, and things just crumbled.

"Despite that, coming home was great, my family still lived here, and growing up here it was great coming back here and playing for your hometown team," Tupa said.

CHAPTER 12

OZZIE NEWSOME

Tight End 1978–1990
The Game: January 4, 1981, vs Oakland Raiders at Cleveland
Stadium
OAKLAND RAIDERS 14—CLEVELAND BROWNS 12

OZZIE NEWSOME ROAMS the sidelines on game days, always remembering where he started—and now, as the current General Manger of the Baltimore Ravens, how far he's come.

He re-defined the position of tight end during his 13 seasons playing for the Browns, being a threat as a receiver, as well as a blocker.

He was a team leader, a player who never missed a game, and remains one of only five players in Browns history to play in parts of three decades.

His career in Cleveland was littered with record-breaking numbers, to the point that when he retired after the 1990 season he had amassed 662 passes for 7,980 yards and 47 touchdowns.

Newsome left the game still playing at a high level. In his final season he still played in all 16 games for the Browns, starting 15 of them. When he did hang up the cleats, he was fourth on the league's all-time list for receptions, and had caught more passes than any tight end.

He paved the way for tight ends like Tony Gonzalez, Shannon Sharpe, Antonio Gates, and even now Rob Gronkowski, to be big parts of their teams' offense.

Notes on Ozzie Newsome

Years Played: 1978–1990
Position: Tight End
Height: 6'2"
Weight: 232
Hometown: Muscle Shoals, AL
Current Residence: Baltimore, MD
Occupation: General Manager of the Baltimore Ravens
Accomplishments: Played for legendary coach Bear Bryant at the University of Alabama. In his four years there, he caught 102 passes for 2,070 yards and 16 touchdowns and is considered the best end in school history. Was the 23rd pick in the 1978 NFL Draft by the Browns and in his first game scored a touchdown on an end around against the San Francisco 49ers. In his stellar 13-year career, he caught 662 passes for 7,980 yards and 74 touchdowns, rushing for two more. Retired after the 1990 season and joined the Browns coaching staff, eventually becoming director of pro personnel. Made history as the NFL's first African-American general manager in 2002 and built the Baltimore Ravens into a powerhouse in the AFC, winning a number of division titles, and eventually winning a Super Bowl when the Ravens beat the San Francisco 49ers in February of 2013.
Nickname: "The Wizard of Oz"

Ozzie Newsome gains 9 yards on his first pass reception in the Browns 41-23 win over the Baltimore Colts on Nov. 28, 1983, in Cleveland. (AP Photo/Ernie Mastroianni)

Born in Muscle Shoals, Alabama, on March 16, 1956, Newsome was raised in nearby Leighton in the northwest part of the state, near the Tennessee border. Ozzie's father, Ozzie "Fats" Newsome Sr., ran a restaurant called "Fats' Café," where the future Hall of Fame tight end learned the meaning of hard work. They got an education at the restaurant, while Newsome's mother, Ethel, ran the Newsome household.

It didn't take long to see that Newsome was a special kind of athlete. He was a three-sport star in high school at Colbert County High, was highly sought after by just about every school, and nearly landed at Auburn, where his high school quarterback ended up.

Instead, he chose Alabama, a school coached at the time by legendary coach Bear Bryant. A visit from the school's first African-American player, John Mitchell, sealed the deal as to where Newsome would be playing his college ball.

It turned into a life-changing decision, for at Alabama he became a star playing the split end spot in the team's wishbone offense. He set records at the school, was twice all-conference in the SEC, and was an All-American and a co-captain in his senior season.

In his four-year college career, Newsome caught 102 passes for 2,070 yards and 16 touchdowns, and Bryant called him the best end in school history, high praise for a school that also boasted Don Hutson.

The Browns scooped up Newsome with one of their two first-round picks in the 1978 draft, making him the 23rd overall pick. He became a star with the team right away, scoring a touchdown on a 33-yard end around in a 24–7 opening day win over the San Francisco 49ers.

His first year with the Browns he started all 16 games, making 38 catches for 589 yards and two touchdowns and scoring two more times rushing the football. He was the first Browns rookie in 25 years to be named the team's Offensive Player of the Year in 1978.

He was even better in his second season, in 1979, earning All-Pro honors while pulling in 55 catches for 781 yards and nine scores for a Browns team that was starting to turn the corner into being a force in the AFC.

By 1980, the Browns offense was coming into its own, led by NFL MVP Brian Sipe, and Newsome was a huge part of it, as well. He caught 51 more passes for the 11–5 Browns, and the city fell in love with the team that came to be known as "The Kardiac Kids."

Week after week, the team had exciting come-from-behind wins, and the club seemed to hit its stride, winning four of its last five to win the AFC Central.

With visions of a trip to the Super Bowl dancing in their heads, the team hosted the wild card Oakland Raiders on a historically cold day in Cleveland, with kickoff coming in at -16 with the wind chill.

Newsome and the Browns had little idea what was going to happen on January 4, 1981, a day that Browns fans still remember to this day with heartache.

The Game

We had some big wins when I played for Cleveland, like the double-overtime playoff against the Jets.

But it's a loss that pops into my head today.

We had a magical season in 1980. The majority of the games we won came on last drives with our offense. Each week someone else would make a play to win a game.

We had confidence that as long as there were not zeroes on the clock we could come back and win. We played so well, we won the division and had a bye the first week of the playoffs.

The week we were off, it was cold, real cold, and we practiced in it some. But we also went to the IX Center and did some work inside.

Since we had practiced some in that cold and we were going to play a West Coast team, the Raiders, we thought we had the psychological advantage.

As it turned out, the Raiders were mentally tough, and they handled what ended up being the coldest game ever played in Cleveland.

It was brutal that day.

The cold, the wind, it was hard to keep your focus on every play, but I think most of us handled it the right way. We had the MVP at quarterback, Brian Sipe, and we moved the ball pretty good all day.

However, we didn't score touchdowns and we missed field goals, and in the end that got us.

Late in the game, our defense made a stop and gave us the ball back. The stage was now set for what we had done all season.

There was a third down play where Brian got me the ball and I had nothing but green in front of me. And, just when I thought I was going to the end zone, (Oakland's) Mike Davis clipped my heel and I went down.

An opportunity lost.

So it was either the two-minute warning or we took a timeout. I do know this, we would all rush over to the sideline and get near the heaters during any timeout.

We were wearing special shoes that we got from Canada. Think they were called "broomballs" and they helped us. We were able to make some cuts on the frozen field.

Brian went to Sam and asked for "Red Right 88," a play we had run successfully all season. The play called for Reggie Rucker and me to line up on the right side and Dave Logan on the left side.

The play usually went to Dave. Reggie and I would go left and run into the flow coming with Logan. In fact, the play really is designed to get Logan the ball.

I beat Mike Davis off the line, and when that happened in the season—beating the safety—Sipe would usually go to me. I knew right away that I was going to get the ball. It was windy and the ball hung in the air for a little while. Just enough for Davis to get his hands on it.

I tried to strip it, but he held on and the rest is history. What happened next was something I'll always remember. That place, which had been as loud as ever that day, went completely silent. I call it the "loudest silence" I've ever heard.

Thus the legend of "Red Right 88." I've seen Mike Davis a few times over the years and he just smiles at me. His team, the Raiders, went on to win the Super Bowl that year.

The Aftermath

Little did the Browns and their fans know that the fateful play, "Red Right 88," would go down in Cleveland folklore as another painful memory for a city starved for a title.

Newsome and the team seemed shell-shocked by the loss. The following season the club started 0–2 and never seemed to get going, losing five of their last six to end the year 5–11.

"I've been asked if that game hurt us the following year. I think it did hurt some of us. But we didn't win the close games in 1981 and we fell back," Newsome said.

The '81 season was a painful reminder that you can't live off the year before, as many of the same Browns that were part of those close wins in 1980 also were part of the tough losses the next season.

"The division was tough—all good, playoff-type teams with the Steelers and Oilers—and the Bengals got really good, and they ended up going to the Super Bowl the following year," Newsome said.

The tough losses in Newsome's career didn't stop there. He was also part of the Browns' playoff losses from 1986 to 1989, when three times the team fell one game short of reaching the Super Bowl.

Following the 1990 season, Newsome had had enough; he left the game as a player, instead joining the Browns as a special assignment scout.

His NFL career saw him catch 662 passes for 7,980 yards and 74 touchdowns, rushing for two more.

He moved up the ranks, learning under new Browns coach at the time, Bill Belichick, getting an understanding of the game from a coach who would go on to win four Super Bowls, and in his last two seasons with the Browns served as their director of pro personnel.

Newsome was on the front lines when Art Modell announced that the Browns were moving to Baltimore in November of 1995.

It was gut-wrenching for Newsome, since he was loyal to Modell but also loved the city he called home for nearly two decades.

He made the move to Baltimore and has been with the team ever since. On November 22, 2002, he made history, being named the team's general manager, the first African-American to be a GM in the NFL.

Newsome's smarts on the football field helped him draft a team that won a Super Bowl in the 2000 season with such homegrown players as Ray Lewis, Jonathan Ogden, and Jamal Lewis.

He's since become one of the best GMs in the NFL and has held the position now for the past 13 seasons, a key part of a Ravens team that won its second Super Bowl in 2013.

While he's reached the pinnacle with the Ravens twice, his love for Cleveland still runs deep, and he stood on the steps of the Pro Football Hall of Fame in 1999 entering the Hall for his accomplishments on the field with the Browns.

Newsome goes down as one of the best tight ends ever to play the game. He made three Pro Bowl teams (1981, 1984, 1985) and was an AP first-team All-Pro in 1984, to go along with being selected as part of the NFL 1980s All-Decade Team.

Newsome ended his career making the position of tight end into something many in the NFL had never seen before.

He took that knowledge on the playing field into the front office and has produced a number of winning season, as well as two Super Bowl titles.

One of the best of all. There will always be a bond between Ozzie Newsome and the Cleveland Browns.

CHAPTER 13

STEVE EVERITT

Center 1993–1995
The Game: September 5, 1993, vs Cincinnati Bengals at
Cleveland Stadium
CLEVELAND BROWNS 27—CINCINNATI BENGALS 14

STEVE EVERITT WAS a throwback player, if there ever was one.

With shards of jersey hanging off his body after fighting for 60 minutes on the Browns' offensive line every Sunday, Everitt was as "no nonsense" a player as you would ever find.

He earned a $5,000 fine for wearing a bandana in the first game the former Browns franchise played in the city of Baltimore.

Everitt was never afraid to speak his mind, talking about how much he disliked David Modell, the son of former Browns owner Art Modell.

Even after the team traded brown for purple, making the move in 1996 from Cleveland to Baltimore, Everitt stuck up for the city that drafted him, and fans in Cleveland loved him for it.

Born in Miami, Everitt played at Southridge High School, where he was a star on the field to the point where the school put him in their Hall of Fame in 1988.

He moved on from the sunny skies of Florida to the grey, and sometimes very cold, skies of Ann Arbor, Michigan, where he played for the University of Michigan from 1989 to 1992, majoring in Fine Arts.

Notes on Steve Everitt

Years Played: 1993–1995
Position: Center
Height: 6'5"
Weight: 310
Hometown: Miami, FL
Current Residence: Sugar Loaf Key, FL
Occupation: Stay-at-home dad for his 6-year-old daughter
Accomplishments: In his high school's Hall of Fame at South-ridge High School. Played in, and started in, all 12 games of his freshman year at Michigan as the team went 10–2 in Bo Schembechler's last season as head coach. Continued at center with the team for three more seasons, including the club's undefeated season in 1992 in which they beat Washington in the Rose Bowl. He was also named to the All-Big Ten Conference team following the season. Was the 14th pick of the 1993 NFL Draft for the Browns. Was the starting center from the opener and started 46 games for the team from 1993 to 1995. He also played in, and started, the club's two playoff games in the 1994 season. After his one year with the newly formed Baltimore Ravens in 1996, he moved on to Philadelphia to play for the Eagles, where he started 45 games for the team from 1997 to 1999. Finished his eight-year NFL career with four games in the 2000 season playing for the St.Louis Rams. Appeared in 103 NFL games, starting in 98 of them in his career.
Nickname: None

Steve Everitt gets ready to snap the ball during game action. (Photo courtesy of Steve Everitt)

His best season came in his final one, when, as a senior, he started all 12 games for the undefeated Wolverines, who went on to play in the Rose Bowl, beating Washington.

For his efforts, Everitt was selected as a first-team player on the 1992 All-Big Ten Conference team.

The Browns, looking to add beef to their already developing offensive line, took Everitt in the first round, 14th pick overall, of the 1993 NFL Draft.

It was a memorable draft experience for Everitt, who recalls the memory well to this day.

"From the first day I was drafted, the fans in my opinion were just crazy," Everitt remembers. "They were even at the facility the night me and my mom flew up; it was awesome."

"I was down in Miami, where I grew up with my family, and I had gone out with my friends, and had a long night, a real long night," Everitt said.

"Once I knew the Browns were going to draft me, we started partying again at my house, and then Bill Belichick calls me and says, 'You know, you have to fly in here tonight, right?' so I put the brakes on the party and flew up with my mom.

"Coach (Kirk) Ferentz met us at the airport. It was just an awesome feeling right from the start."

Fans took to Everitt right away. They loved his grit and determination and right away felt that the center was ready to lead the Browns back into being a contender.

"Coming from Michigan and having that rabid fan base, I thought there was nothing close to that, except for Cleveland, their fan base, it was as close as I can think of, the Dawg Pound, just a blue collar city you want to go out and bleed for," Everitt said.

"It was a perfect match from the get-go."

The Browns didn't exactly plan on having Everitt start on the line day one. The team had brought in former Chicago Bears Super Bowl-winning center Jay Hilgenberg in 1992, and he was expected to show Everitt the ropes.

It didn't work out as Everitt had thought. The Browns felt that their first-round pick had done enough to earn the starting job at center, and they released Hilgenberg at the end of training camp.

"I got a taste of the business aspect of the NFL my first training camp. I was playing with Jay Hilgenberg as my mentor, kind of showing me the ropes and what to do, and once they realized that I could handle the job they went ahead and released him," Everitt remembers.

"So the dude that was kind of holding my hand and showing me along was suddenly gone, and now the job was in my lap.

"It was a sweet show of confidence on their part, which made me feel good, but it was pretty heavy at the time."

Entering 1993, not many felt the Browns were going to do all that much better than the season before, when the team won seven games, but Everitt recalls that with head coach Bill Belichick the Browns had big plans for the season.

"I thought we were gonna go win the Super Bowl my rookie year," Everitt recalls. "We shot out the gate we were 3–0, and then 4–2, and everything was looking up, it started out wonderfully."

It did start out great for the Browns, and the 1993 season began with an opening day affair at Cleveland Stadium against a division rival, the Cincinnati Bengals.

The Game

I can't imagine another season, just the fact that it was my rookie year was going to make it crazy for me.

Walking out on that field at Cleveland Stadium for the first time in a regular season game, it's a whole other level; the preseason really doesn't prepare you for it.

Any veteran telling you what to expect doesn't prepare you for it. I usually liked to go out on the field early.

I liked to go out four to five hours early. I didn't want there to be any surprises. I wanted to get over the hyperventilating and the panic attacks.

It seemed like the field was the greenest green I had ever seen, the fans were the loudest fans I had ever heard; it was just overwhelming and awesome.

We opened my rookie year at home against Cincinnati, and three hours before the game I'm in the locker room and Bernie shows up, and he wanted to go over a couple of last-minute adjustments.

I was sitting there with him going over some calls and protections with him, and I kind of had to excuse myself because it was hitting me that Bernie Kosar was my quarterback, that I was getting ready to go out to play an NFL game with him!

So I excuse myself and go throw up, and this is all three hours before my first game. I even caught myself staring at Bernie putting his uniform on, and I was starstruck and had to keep talking myself down.

I grew up in Miami and worshipped the Hurricanes, and Bernie was my idol, and now he's my freaking quarterback; you couldn't write that.

I remember sitting on the bench a few hours before the game, and just sitting there and you get a chance to reflect on what got you here. You remember all the people that helped you along the way.

There was another factor, though, in the pregame, and that was having known I was going up against (Bengals nose tackle) Tim Krumrie; he was an iconic figure, that was making me nervous.

Our strength coach when I was at Michigan was Mike Gittleson, an iconic weight and strength coach, and while I was at Michigan he brought Krumrie in to talk to us about lifting, and lifting in season.

I remember thinking how strong his hands were the first time I had met him five years earlier, when I was a 230-pound freshman weakling at Michigan. He had the strongest grip strength you had ever come across, and it wasn't by accident.

I can remember taking stuff that Krumrie taught us in college, and fast forward to my first start in the NFL and I'm playing against him!

He got a sack on me in the first quarter of the first game I ever played, and I'm ready to fall apart, get pissed, and just start fighting everybody.

But I held it together, and we ended up running the ball pretty good that game. In the first half he got the better of me, but in the second half I actually made some plays against him.

I was able to keep him off the line and our backfield. I don't think he had too many tackles; he did have the sack on me and I always dwell on that.

I remember overthinking things in the first quarter, and early on in the game just trying not to get too caught up in the moment, and just blow all your energy before the first quarter is even over.

We had a great training camp that year, and I had to go back to not forgetting my fundamentals.

Crazy stuff goes through your head when you are dealing with an unknown, but really that day you couldn't have written a better script for that first game.

After the game I wanted to stay on the field and take it all in, but I was getting a full body cramp, so I had to go get IVs after the game.

I pushed through it, do what I was taught to do, and sometimes things work out.

The Aftermath

The 1993 season will be remembered by Browns fans as one of the most frustrating in franchise history.

The club started out 5–2, with an exciting 28–23 win over the Pittsburgh Steelers at home on October 24th.

They headed into the bye with things looking up, but an injury to quarterback Vinny Testaverde set up a decision that rocked the franchise.

Kosar got the start at quarterback for the game after the bye, and the team was dominated, 29–14, by old rival John Elway and the Denver Broncos.

The Browns' fan favorite quarterback was sacked six times, and as legend goes he drew up a play in the dirt that resulted in a touchdown in the final seconds to wide out Michael Jackson.

The day after the Denver loss, Belichick uttered the famous line about Kosar having "diminishing skills," and the nine-year vet was released.

It sent shock waves through the city and the team, and they never recovered.

"Things started rolling, and that just grounded to a crazy halt after that Denver game," Everitt recalls.

The team went from a 5–3 contender in the AFC to an afterthought, as they dropped six of their last eight games and ended the year 7–9.

While it was a tough season, the club recovered to reach the postseason in 1994, going 11–5 behind a line led by Everitt, and a great season by their veteran-led defense.

It seemed, once more, as if things were on the up, but again the rug was pulled out under the players when midway through the 1995 season Art Modell announced that the team was moving to Baltimore following that season.

Everitt made the move to Baltimore and played there for one season before moving on to play three more seasons for the Philadelphia Eagles.

He played in four games for the St. Louis Rams in 2000 before leaving the game for good.

Everitt's first season in the pros will still be recalled as his most memorable, the time when he got a first-hand look at what the NFL was all about.

Good and bad.

"I was subjected to all the things that rookies had to go through," Everitt said. "But I had guys like Hilgenberg, Bernie, and even Tony Jones, they were kind of looking out for me.

"They didn't let me get screwed with like they did some rookies, I just felt like part of the group."

CHAPTER 14

TIM COUCH

Quarterback 1999–2003
The Game: October 27, 2002, vs New York Jets at Giants
Stadium
CLEVELAND BROWNS 24—NEW YORK JETS 21

WHEN THE EXPANSION Cleveland Browns were given the number one pick in the 1999 NFL Draft, the choices came down primarily to two players, both of whom were quarterbacks.

The first was a big-play, hard-throwing quarterback from the University of Oregon, Akili Smith. He was expected to be a "can't miss," a player who would be both dynamic and be able to make sensational plays.

The other was Tim Couch, who set numerous passing records while leading the University of Kentucky to a 7–5 record his senior season in 1998, and a battle in the Outback Bowl against Penn State.

Browns brass kept a close eye on both players leading up to the draft, putting both through a variety of workouts before coming to a decision that Couch would be the player the team would bank its future on as the team came back into the NFL.

Couch walked on stage in New York on April 17th, 1999, holding up a Browns jersey with a smile on his face as Browns fans had visions of their next great quarterback coming into the fold.

"It was an honor to play in Cleveland, such a storied franchise, especially with the way I came into the league with it being the

Notes on Tim Couch

Years Played: 1999–2003
Position: Quarterback
Height: 6'4"
Weight: 225
Hometown: Hyden, KY
Current Residence: Lexington, KY
Occupation: Television Talent for SEC Football Games
Accomplishments: Attended Leslie County High School in Hyden, Kentucky. While in high school, set four national high school records: most pass completions (872), passing yardage (12,104), touchdown passes (132), and passing percentage for a season (75.1). Was Kentucky's Mr. Football in 1995. Also played basketball in high school, scoring 3,023 points in his career. Threw for 8,772 yards and 76 touchdowns in three years as the starter for Kentucky. Led the University of Kentucky to the Outback Bowl in 1998, falling to Penn State. Was First-team All-SEC, First-team All-American, and SEC Player of the Year in 1998. Had a career quarterback rating in the NFL of 75.1, going 22–37 as a starter for the Browns from 1999 to 2003. Married to former Playboy Playmate and Akron, Ohio, native Heather Kozar; the couple have two children, Chase and Brady.
Nickname: None

Tim Couch signals down the line during a game against the St. Louis Rams in St. Louis on Oct. 24, 1999. (AP Photo/James A. Finley)

Browns' first year back, and being the first player they picked in the draft," Couch recalls.

The 1999 season was supposed to be one in which Couch learned the quarterback position at the NFL level, playing behind veteran Ty Detmer.

Instead, Couch was thrown into the fire right away. After an opening night 43–0 loss at home to the rival Pittsburgh Steelers, the first overall pick in the draft was given the keys to the Browns offense and was named the starting quarterback moving forward.

Some felt that Couch's quick insertion into the starting lineup doomed him for failure, more so playing behind an offensive line that had issues keeping the quarterback upright.

"I think at the time, every player feels like they are ready to go and play, and I think I would have been; had I been on a more veteran team with more experience, I think I could have gone in and played okay as a rookie," Couch said.

But Couch and the team had their issues, and the Browns started out 0–7 before finally getting their first win on Halloween afternoon, October 31, against the New Orleans Saints in New Orleans.

The first pick ended that first season throwing for 15 touchdowns and 13 interceptions, with a quarterback rating of 73.2.

"I did gain a lot of experience, and I felt like I did grow quite a bit throughout the season," Couch said of his rookie campaign.

"It was tough, though; I broke the all-time sack record that season. I got sacked 56 times, so I took a beating, but I wouldn't trade it for anything."

The following season, Couch played in just seven games before breaking his thumb on the final play of practice leading up to a week-eight game against the Steelers.

The next year, the team started 6–4 under new coach Butch Davis and finished the year 7–9, but with hopes of finally turning the corner.

In 2002, Couch had his best season of his NFL career, as he and the Browns made their only playoff appearance since the franchise had rejoined the NFL in 1999.

The team started 2–4, and after a home win over the Houston Texans to get to 3–4, the team traveled to Giants Stadium for a big week-eight game against the Jets.

They did so with heavy hearts, however: four days before they took the field against the Jets, Browns owner Al Lerner passed away from brain cancer.

The Game

The game in Pittsburgh in 1999 comes to mind, but the one for me is a game that probably no one would think of, but it was the year we went to the playoffs, 2002. We played the Jets on the road, and it was the game after Mr. Lerner died.

We went to New York, were down 15 points at halftime, and we came out and I played one of the best games I ever played, and we really just played well in the second half.

Our defense played great in the second half, created some turnovers, and we ended up winning the game, and it was a huge, huge turning point for us that season to eventually help get us to the playoffs.

We were down, 21–6, at the half, and nothing really memorable got said at halftime, but we just came out a little bit flat that day, we were all emotionally drained, we had been to Mr. Lerner's funeral earlier in the week, and we just came out a little bit flat.

We came out of the locker room at half, and our defense made a couple quick stops, and we got a touchdown on the board when I hit Mark Campbell to make it 21–13, and we just kept the momentum going from there.

I was able to get pretty hot there in the second half. I threw for close to 300 yards in the game, and we had receivers making plays all over the field, and it was just a really fun game to be a part of.

Anytime you go on the road and win a game it's special, especially when you are down like we were down at the half and you rally back. It was one of the more memorable wins for me.

That win was so special. I remember being in the locker room after the game, and everyone was so emotional because of Mr. Lerner's passing.

Mr. Lerner's son, Randy, was in the locker room and he gave a speech, and Carmen Policy spoke, and it was just an emotional time for us, and it was a great way to go out and honor him and get that win for him.

I remember leaving the field that day feeling so proud, and you could see the look on Randy's face when we walked in that locker room.

He was just so happy, not just because we got a win, but you could see he was still mourning the loss of his father, understandably so.

Coach Davis got up and gave an emotional speech, and he was crying during his speech, very emotional, and I think there probably wasn't a dry eye in the locker room, to be honest.

We were all not only happy to get the win, but happy for the Lerner family that we could give them that win on that day after the passing of Mr. Lerner.

It was a special time, an emotional locker room, and an emotional plane ride back to Cleveland. It was a great win for us.

We won seven out of our last ten games in the regular season that year to make the playoffs. That game against the Jets got us to 4–4; it really got us on the right track.

That was the same season when in December, I threw a Hail Mary on the last play down in Jacksonville to Quincy Morgan to win us that game, and so there was a lot of close games down the stretch.

I remember a lot of games coming down to the wire. We lost a couple but we won some, too; it was crazy.

We beat Baltimore that year in late December to get us to 8–7 on the road on a last-minute drive. I threw a touchdown with 29 seconds left to Mark Campbell, and there was just some great wins that year, a real memorable year.

The Aftermath

While 2002 was a very up-and-down season for the Browns, the win over the Ravens in week 16 led to a home game against the Atlanta Falcons in week 17 that would decide if they would make the postseason.

Atlanta, with up-and-coming superstar Michael Vick, had already clinched a playoff berth, and the Browns scored 14 fourth-quarter points to pull out a 17–16 win to reach the postseason.

It was a bittersweet win for Couch, as on the first play of the second quarter he broke his leg and missed the emotional win to reach the playoffs, as well as the AFC Wild Card game the following week against the Steelers in Pittsburgh.

"Looking back, it's kind of how my career went. Every time I got ready to make that next step and climb that ladder and take it to the next level, something would knock me back a little bit," Couch said.

"Being such a young player, and taking such a young team to the playoffs, I really felt I was on the right track. Then I break my leg against the Falcons in the game we had to win to make the playoffs."

The game in Pittsburgh turned out to be another turning point in the franchise, as Kelly Holcomb playing in place of Couch torched the Steelers secondary for 429 yards and three touchdowns.

The Browns, who led at one point, 24–7, gave up the lead and the game late, falling 36–33 in the final minute.

Davis, though, was so impressed with Holcomb that he declared the quarterback position would be up for grabs during training camp the following season.

Holcomb was named the starter for opening day, and it threw the entire 2003 season into a tailspin for the young Browns off their playoff appearance the season before.

"That season was kind of a wash. Kelly would start a couple of games, I would start a couple of games, we were both miserable," Couch said.

"I just didn't understand coach Davis's decision to do that, especially after we had such a successful season the year before.

"Anytime you have a quarterback controversy the locker room is going to be split, and I think that year it kind of tore the team apart, and not only was it the end of my career but the end of his coaching tenure in Cleveland, as well."

Couch left Cleveland after 2003, and the team with quarterback Jeff Garcia went in a different direction, letting their first pick of their expansion franchise walk.

"When I left Cleveland, I got a great opportunity to go to Green Bay and be Brett Favre's backup and potentially be his replacement when he retires . . . and I tear my shoulder apart," Couch recalls.

"I had a torn rotator cuff and torn labrum and a torn bicep, so I had my whole shoulder repaired, was trying to make a comeback, and I tore my rotator cuff again.

"After the second surgery, I literally wasn't even close to being the same player I was, so it was kind of done at that point."

Couch's career ended with his playing in 62 games, starting 59, and in those starts going 22–37. He threw for 11,131 career yards, with 64 touchdowns, 67 interceptions, and a QB rating of 75.1.

Despite the way things ended with the Browns, Couch still recalls his time in Cleveland with fondness.

"It was an honor to get to play in front of that fan base that was so starved to get football back in Cleveland," Couch said.

"It was awesome and a lot of fun. Even though we were an expansion team and very young, and we were not winning very many football games, it was still such a cool experience because the fans were so excited to get us back on the field and to have a team to cheer for.

"I remember feeling a lot of pressure being the face of the new franchise and being so young, but I have great memories of being there in Cleveland, I loved my time there and am still a Browns fan to this day."

CHAPTER 15

DICK AMBROSE

Linebacker 1975–1983
The Game: September 24, 1979, vs Dallas Cowboys at Cleveland Stadium
CLEVELAND BROWNS 26—DALLAS COWBOYS 7

FOR THE PAST 12 years, Dick Ambrose has had people stand and rise when he enters the room, as he now dons the robe of a judge in Cuyahoga County Court of Common Pleas.

His second career followed that of being a linebacker for the Cleveland Browns for nine seasons, playing at linebacker and earning the nickname "Bam-Bam," after the character on the popular TV cartoon, *The Flintstones.*

Born and raised in New Rochelle, New York, Ambrose played his high school ball at Iona Prep and moved on to the University of Virginia, where he shined and earned All-ACC honors in both his junior and senior seasons.

Despite the honors, Ambrose fell all the way to the 12th round of the 1975 NFL Draft, when he was the 290th pick, joining a Browns team that was coming off a 4–10 season in 1974.

"There were some tough times when I first came to the team in 1975," Ambrose recalls.

"The team had just fired (head coach) Nick Skorich, and Forest Gregg was a brand new head coach, and I'm fresh out of college and don't really know what to expect.

Notes on Dick Ambrose

Years Played: 1975–1983
Position: Linebacker
Height: 6'0"
Weight: 235
Hometown: New Rochelle, NY
Current Residence: Westlake, OH
Occupation: Judge in Cuyahoga County
Accomplishments: Was an All-ACC for his junior and senior seasons at Virginia. Was a 12th round pick of the Browns in 1975, the 290th pick overall in the NFL Draft. Played for nine seasons for the Browns, playing middle linebacker, right inside linebacker, and left inside linebacker. He tallied five interceptions with nine fumble recoveries in his professional career. Started as a rookie and was the team's most valuable defensive player in 1977. Ambrose was honored in 1981 by his teammates with the "Captain's Award," given to that team member who is "A worker, a team player, and an inspiration." He started 64 consecutive games before breaking his leg in a game against the New York Jets in 1983 and spent the 1984 season, his last, on injured reserve. Ambrose and his wife, Mary Beth, live in Westlake with their three children, Rachel, Karen, and Kristy.
Nickname: Bam-Bam

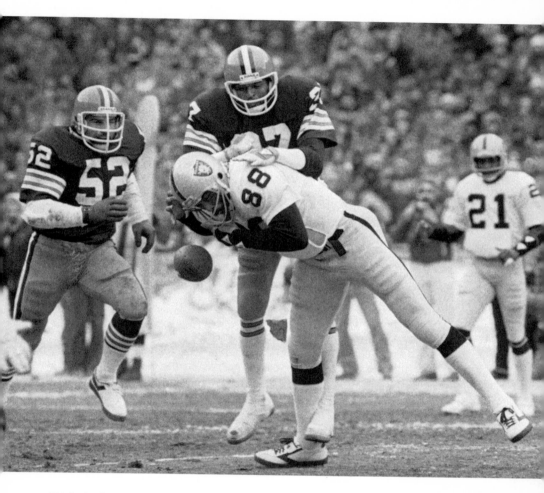

Dick Ambrose (52) moves in as Thom Darden breaks up a play against the Raiders. (AP Photos)

"I was kind of overwhelmed by the size and speed of the guys at the NFL level. I was just trying to make adjustments, and trying to make the best impression I could at the time."

Ambrose made the team and made an impact right away, thanks in part to a new coaching staff that was willing to give some of the newer players and rookies on the team a shot from day one.

The first season under Gregg was not an easy one. Back in those days, training camps were brutal, with players often having to go full pads under the sun in the hottest days of the summer.

Players were also often required to take the field up to three times per day, not to mention meetings and outside work, to get ready for the season.

"It was a really, really hard training camp, nothing like it is today," Ambrose remembers. "It was more like the Bataan Death March than like training camp is today.

"Somehow we managed to survive, for those of us that made the team, and I was fortunate enough to make the team, and then kind of evolve from there as the years moved forward. In that first training camp in 1975, we had live contact virtually every practice, and back then we had six preseason games.

"So we had six weeks of preseason games, and another two weeks before we played our first preseason game, and the rookies came in a week early for rookie camp.

"So we had about nine weeks of practice before the regular season even started. Most of us who were used to an 11-game college season were almost worn out before the season even started."

That rookie season in 1975, Ambrose played in all 14 games, starting ten as the Browns struggled to a 3–11 mark in Gregg's first season.

Despite the growing pains, Ambrose was able to get his feet wet because the coaches believed in him enough to give him a chance to play a lot that first season in Cleveland.

"Fortunately, or maybe not fortunately for me, there had been a change in the coaching staff so no one really had an institutional history there, so no one could really rely on that, and everyone had to prove themselves," Ambrose said.

"Even established veteran players were put under the microscope by this new coaching staff. So it gave a rookie a much better opportunity to make the team, which I did."

That first season Ambrose developed a reputation for being an all-out player, going 100 percent on each and every play, both in games as well as in practice.

It's part of the reason behind the "Bam-Bam" nickname that he developed that first season in Cleveland.

"In trying to make the best impression and put my best foot forward, I went all out in practice, hitting guys as hard as I could," Ambrose said.

"Veterans would pick on rookies a lot, and they would have pet names for you for nicknames or things like that, so that's how the 'Bam-Bam' nickname got in there. It was going to be between 'Bam-Bam' or 'Barney Rubble,' and they decided on 'Bam-Bam.'

"I thought that was a much better name for a linebacker. It kind of stuck after that first year, and kind of fit my style of play."

The 1976 season saw the Browns take a big step forward, going 9–5, but still finishing third in the very competitive AFC Central.

The team went backwards in 1977, going 6–8, as Gregg was fired just before the end of the season, opening the door for Sam Rutigliano to come in to coach the team to start the 1978 campaign.

"We kind of got a little bit better under Forrest, but there was no real continuity to the team at that point," Ambrose said.

"We had a new coach in three years with Sam Rutigliano, and it was a different coaching style, but one that believed in us.

"For me I thought it was refreshing. I liked it, a lot of the other guys liked it. We got a little bit group of players in the draft, and we started to win a little bit more consistently. The 1979 season was really the start of the turnaround."

The team went 8–8 in Rutigliano's first season, setting the stage for the 1979 season in which the team finally started to put pieces in place to be a force in the NFL.

The 1979 season saw the Browns jump off to a 3–0 start, winning all three games by three points each.

It set the stage for a week-four prime-time showdown with a team that won the NFC the season before, the team known by many as "America's Team," the Dallas Cowboys.

The Game

It's really hard to pick out one game that is better than all the rest. The playoff game in January of 1981 was certainly memorable, but there were others, as well.

On a more positive note, the positive memory I have that really typifies the town and the type of team we had was the 1979 game we had against Dallas on a Monday night in week four.

We were 3–0, and they were 3–0, so it was a battle of unbeaten teams, and it was a big stage, that being *Monday Night Football*.

I just remember how electric the crowd was, just driving down to the game listening on the radio to all the people calling into the sports talk shows; people were really psyched up for this game.

You couldn't help but be enthusiastic since it seemed to be across the whole town. During the game, you obviously knew it was going to be a hard-fought game.

Those types of games, those types of nights are special.

When you are walking through the tunnel through that stadium, to the dugout, and mind you it is a tunnel, you can only walk single file though the tunnel, and the lights in there are very dim, and you are walking out to darkness before you see the light of the stadium lights.

You kind of symbolically rise up out of that darkness and lowness onto the field level, and as soon as the fans see an orange helmet poke out of that tunnel, they go crazy.

You can hear the first guy walking out if you are not the first guy, which I never was, and you just hear the roar of the fans as you walk out that tunnel, and that would send chills down your spine.

I always remember the touchdown pass to Ozzie Newsome, it was in the first quarter. We had come off the field after we held them and they were forced to punt, and our offense was out there.

A couple of plays went on, and I'm standing on the sidelines, and sometimes you don't really notice what's going on out on the field if you're on the sideline catching a break or going over some game planning concepts.

It just so happened that the players in front of me from where I was on the bench, there was some open air space and I could see directly onto the field, and I managed to look up and saw Ozzie running downfield, and he had a couple yards on the defender, who was probably Cliff Harris or Charlie Waters.

He's just standing there looking back for the ball, and I could see it perfectly and I just see the ball floating down into his hands, and he steps across the goal line, and the place just exploded in a roar like nothing I have ever heard.

I had heard that place roar a million times, but it just seemed different this time for some reason. It was really exciting.

It was the type of game where throughout it was really high energy for everybody, and we won.

On the defensive side, I don't recall anything specific we were trying to attack or any of their weaknesses, but I remember how very focused we were in practice all week leading up to the game, because it was Dallas, because it was Monday night, and because we had an extra day of practice.

We had come off some games in which we were tough before then, too, we were not coasting through the season by any means.

Our first three wins were all by three points. We had beat the Jets to start the season in overtime, then won by three at Kansas City, and the week before in our home opener we beat the Colts by three.

133

Going into this game against Dallas we were not even favored, and I think it was one of those things where we got on our work clothes and decided to do the job.

Really, any game, if you don't spend the time in practice paying attention, and paying attention to every detail, it's not going to show up any better at the game.

You just can't turn on the switch on Sunday, or in this case Monday, you have to put in the effort during the week.

We were beginning to learn that in 1979, that's why I think it paid dividends in 1980.

I wouldn't say we were intimidated by Dallas, but when you are playing an opponent that everyone says is superior, you look at it as a challenge.

If you are intimated, I think that's a challenge you back down from.

When you are facing stiff odds like that, and you are bound and determined to face those odds and let the chips fall where they may, then you're not intimidated, you're focused, and you're going to do your best.

More often than not, the team that makes fewer mistakes is going to win, no matter who you are. Usually, chance favors the prepared mind; that is what I think happened that night.

We wanted it maybe a little bit more, and maybe we prepared a little bit better. That's usually what it boils down to.

The Aftermath

The 1979 campaign saw the Browns go 9–7. They started the year 4–0, and were 6–3 at one point, but lost four of their last six games to end any hopes of a playoff berth.

Even with that, the pieces started to fall in place for the Browns, and it set up one of the most memorable seasons in franchise history in 1980.

"The '79 team really laid the foundation for that '80 team, and any winning team, any winning season, it does not happen overnight," Ambrose said.

"You can't just get one or two different players and you're a totally different team. You do have to build, and even if you do get one or two players, we did get Calvin Hill and Lyle Alzado in the prior years, all of which helped, but there still has to be a maturing process, and the team has to gel together, and people need to know each other."

The 1980 season will forever be remembered as the season of the famous "Kardiac Kids," with thrilling comebacks and last-second wins for the Browns, who went 11–5 and won the AFC Central for the first time since 1971.

The heartbreak of the season came on January 4, 1981, when the Browns lost the game known as "Red Right 88," a divisional playoff loss to the Oakland Raiders, 14–12, in sub-zero temps on the Lakefront.

Ambrose played through 1983, playing in a total of 116 games for the Browns, starting in 103.

The linebacker was already thinking about his life after football while still in his playing days. While a member of the Browns, he started law school.

He began practicing law when he graduated from Cleveland-Marshall College of Law in 1987 at the age of 34.

He took the bench for the Cuyahoga County Court of Common Pleas in 2004 and has been a success in his law career following a successful career with the Browns.

CHAPTER 16

BRIAN BRENNAN

Wide Receiver 1984–1991
The Game: January 11, 1987, vs Denver Broncos at Cleveland Stadium
DENVER BRONCOS 23—CLEVELAND BROWNS 20

IN THE HISTORY of Cleveland sports, no game leaves a sting quite like that of the 1986 AFC Championship Game between the Cleveland Browns and Denver Broncos.

The excitement of the Browns and their fans was at a fever pitch for the game, one that represented their football team's advance to the franchise's first Super Bowl.

Instead, after a 98-yard series of plays that to this day is known simply as "The Drive," generated by John Elway and the Broncos to tie the game in regulation, and then a controversial field goal in overtime, Browns fans were left stunned, missing out on their best chance ever to reach a Super Bowl.

One player who saw it firsthand was then third-year wide receiver Brian Brennan, who during the game made what could have gone down as a signature play that looked as though it would send the team to the Super Bowl.

The play was a 48-yard touchdown grab from quarterback Bernie Kosar with fewer than six minutes to go and gave the Browns a 20–13 lead.

Brennan's catch, and march into the end zone past Dennis Smith, appeared to put the Browns in position for a win. Little did

Notes on Brian Brennan

Years Played: 1984–1991
Position: Wide Receiver
Height: 5'9"
Weight: 178
Hometown: Bloomfield, Michigan
Current Residence: Pepper Pike, OH
Occupation: Managing Director at Key Bank
Accomplishments: In three seasons with Boston College, caught 115 passes for 2,180 yards and 14 touchdowns. Won the Scanlan Award his senior season at Boston College, given to the senior football player who is outstanding in scholarship, leadership, and athletic ability. In his best game with the Browns, pulled in seven catches for 176 yards and a touchdown in the regular season finale against San Diego on December 21, 1986. In eight seasons with the Browns he had 315 catches, with 20 touchdowns. In his NFL career, pulled in 334 receptions, 4,338 yards and scored 20 TDs in 132 NFL games. In ten playoff games, caught 24 passes for 329 yards and four touchdowns. A member of the Greater Cleveland Sports Hall of Fame.
Nickname: None

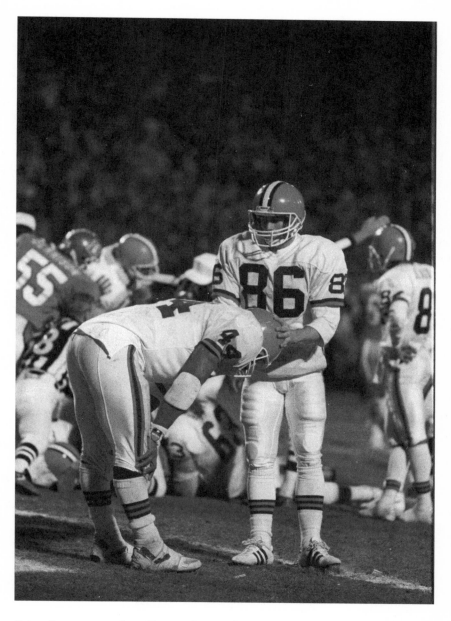

Brian Brennan comforts Earnest Byner after "The Fumble" against the Denver Broncos in the closing minutes of the 1987-88 AFC Championship game. (AP Photo/Mark Duncan)

they know the magic Elway would have that fateful afternoon in Cleveland.

During the Browns' glory years of the 1980s, Brennan was as consistent a receiver as the team had.

He might not have been as flashy as fellow wide outs Webster Slaughter and Reggie Langhorne, but he earned the trust of Kosar and in the two seasons of '86 and '87 hauled in 98 catches for 12 touchdowns.

One of six children, Brennan was a successful wide receiver at Brother Rice High School in Michigan. He moved on to Boston College to continue his education, and to play college football.

Brennan had a solid college career, catching passes from playmaking quarterback Doug Flutie. In his college career, he caught 115 passes for 2,180 yards and 14 touchdowns, catching 66 passes for 1,149 yards with eight touchdowns in his senior season alone.

After being selected by the Browns in the fourth round of the 1984 draft, he started just four games his rookie season but was active as a punt returner, averaging eight yards a return on 25 kicks.

After starting ten games his second season, he was a big piece of the offense by his third season, as the Browns were on their way to one of the best regular seasons in their history, winning 12 of 16 games and going into the playoffs as the AFC's number one seed.

That year, he caught 55 passes for 838 yards and six touchdowns, and the Browns had the look of a champion, only to be derailed by the most crushing loss in franchise history.

The Game

The best team did not win.

I think most people thought the Jets or the Browns were the two best teams in the AFC; then the Broncos were there, too.

Once we got by the Jets, we felt very confident about beating the Denver Broncos. That's the first thing I remember when I think about that AFC Championship Game leading up to it.

The City of Cleveland itself was so energized for the game, and it meant even more hosting the game.

Everyone remembers 1981, the "Red Right 88" playoff loss to Oakland, so it had been a while since we were in such a big game, and even more so at home.

I can remember one of the restaurants, Hyde Park Grille, had a steak on the menu called the "Brennan." There was another menu with "Lobster Langhorne" after wide out Reggie Langhorne, and Bernie Kosar had a food item, as well.

Then came the "Bernie, Bernie" song, and you could feel the energy of the city. It was a special time for me as a player, and it sure seemed like a special time for the fans in general.

We really felt like we had the best team.

I recall the media, and Denver was making a big deal about the receivers on the Broncos. They had what was called the "Three Amigos": Ricky Nattiel, Vance Johnson, and Mark Jackson.

Our wide receiver core was Webster Slaughter, Langhorne, and as the third receiver, me. We felt we were much better as a group, for sure.

I remember the police officers surrounding the field. I remember the painted grass on the field at old Cleveland Stadium.

In that game, we were the better team. We got up on them, and of course they came back with "The Drive," but that crowd, you could feel it, every play mattered.

It was hard to think that any one play didn't matter; the crowd was so into it, they were electric.

The Super Bowl was in Pasadena that year, and everybody kept talking about Pasadena, so we just thought all along we would be in Pasadena.

I'm not sure what our offensive coordinator, Lindy Infante, or Bernie Kosar were looking to do, but I remember being lined up against Broncos safety Dennis Smith a lot. I kept telling Bernie, "Hey, I got Dennis Smith on me."

I don't remember the exact scene of the play call, or the exact strategy. I recall the play, though. We scored what we thought was going to be the go-ahead touchdown.

The name of the play was "Two Flip Y, Y Option X Smash." On my side, Webster Slaughter ran a delayed, what we called a "smash" route, he was the "X" receiver.

I was going to run a post-corner route. On the other side, Reggie Langhorne was the "Y," and he was going to run the "Y" option.

It was a one-on-one situation, and it was me against Dennis Smith. We kind of talked about it, and Bernie kind of looked at me, and we made eye contact. I really felt he was coming to me.

There was some pressure on the play, on Bernie, and the ball was kind of underthrown, and he found me in the slot, and I had to come back a little bit and find the ball.

I almost came back so far that Dennis Smith almost ran past me. He lost his balance, and I caught the ball expecting him to be there. He was kind of stumbling.

I didn't know which way to go around him, right or left, and I finally chose left, and I ran into the end zone, with a lot of room to spare.

It was a real big moment for me, obviously.

That moment was still younger in my career, and maybe many people still thought of me as Doug Flutie's favorite receiver kind of player.

Here I had the chance to make the big play, without Doug Flutie anywhere around.

I came back after the touchdown on the sidelines, and Gary Danielson, who was a good friend at the time, and he and I were both Detroit boys.

He went to a Catholic school called Dearborn Divine Child, and I went to Brother Rice, and here the two of us, from Detroit, were almost shaking on the sidelines from excitement, really think we were going to the Super Bowl.

We had kept John Elway down for most of the game, then lickety-split, Ken Bell bobbles the kickoff and they have to start on their two-yard line.

So they have to go 98 yards for Elway, and for whatever reason the coaches chose to go into the prevent defense, rather than keeping guys like Dave Puzzuoli and others attacking John Elway.

We kind of got conservative, way conservative, too conservative, and it was history, and John Elway was just too good in those pressure situations.

It was really hard to be on the sidelines. So disappointing, and so hard to watch. Play after play, third-and-18 he hits Mark Jackson for 20 yards, and then I remember Sammy Winder with some big plays, and Steve Sewell with a couple plays.

Then Carl Hairston just missed tipping that ball when he threw it into the end zone to Mark Jackson for the touchdown. It was so hard to watch.

We still had 39 seconds to go after they scored, but it was bad play after bad play, and we ended up going into overtime.

Going into overtime, they had the momentum for sure, and we were somewhat dismayed. We were just trying to regroup a bit, everything happened so quickly.

We were on our heels and they were on their toes, and we ended up sputtering out a little bit, and they made enough plays to get into field goal range.

There's a long tunnel between the field at old Cleveland Municipal Stadium and the locker room. It was a long, quiet walk.

Kind of like a funeral, there was such a sense of sadness; it was really very hard to digest what had just happened.

The Aftermath

If the Browns and their fans had a hard time with the loss in the 1986 AFC Championship Game, the finish of the 1987 AFC Championship Game was just as crushing.

A year after "The Drive," the team again had a successful 1987 campaign, beat the Indianapolis Colts in the Divisional Playoff game, and then traveled to Denver for a rematch with the Broncos.

The team fell behind the Broncos, 21–3, at the half, but by late in the fourth quarter trailed, 38–31, and were driving for the tying score.

That's when the next heartbreak of Cleveland sports took place, a play that is still known as "The Fumble." Browns running back Earnest Byner was stripped and fumbled as he was at about the Broncos' 5-yard line trying to make it to the end zone.

The Browns fell, 38–33, and again it was a crushing way to end the season. The team made the playoffs the following season, falling to Houston in the AFC Wild Card Game on Christmas Eve, and then coach Marty Schottenheimer and the team parted ways.

In 1989, the club under Bud Carson again made it to the AFC Title Game but again lost to the Broncos, this time by a score of 37–21, ending the team's best run at a chance for a Super Bowl appearance, despite reaching the AFC Title Game three times in four seasons.

Following the 1989 AFC Title loss to Denver, Brennan stayed with the Browns for two more seasons, catching 76 passes in his last two years with the team.

He played nine games with the Bengals and six with the Chargers in 1992, before walking away from the NFL following the '92 season.

Brennan always stayed close to the City of Cleveland, and his second career took him into the finance industry, as the Managing Director and Division Head for Fixed Income within KeyBanc Capital Markets.

Many Browns fans of the 1980s and early '90s still say Brennan is their favorite Browns player of that time.

His on-field grit and determination was something that fans recall to this day, as well as his ability to come through in the clutch.

While the 1986 AFC Title Game didn't go the Browns' way, Brennan's touchdown catch to this day is one of the favorite memories of Browns fans worldwide.

CHAPTER 17

JOSH CRIBBS

Wide Receiver 2005–2012
The Game: December 10, 2009, vs Pittsburgh Steelers at
Browns Stadium
CLEVELAND BROWNS 13—PITTSBURGH STEELERS 6

THE CLEVELAND BROWNS had plenty of issues winning games during Josh Cribbs's eight seasons with the team, but he always gave it everything he had. His is the ultimate underdog story after going undrafted out of local MAC school Kent State in 2005.

While fans were pulling for him from day one, not many could have assumed he would turn into a face of the franchise for much of his time in Cleveland.

Many would assume that not getting drafted would have been an insult, but to Cribbs it was just part of the business in the NFL.

"I needed to not get drafted, to give me that chip on my shoulder, that boost of motivation," Cribbs recalls.

"My potential was there. I was capable and I was willing. But I needed that extra motivation to put me over the edge, to play in such a way that it would like make people think I was drafted. People will even come up to me today and say, 'What round were you drafted in?'"

By the time it was all said and done, Cribbs certainly didn't fit the profile of an undrafted player. He was a four-time AFC Special Teams Player of the Week, the NFL Alumni Special Teams Player of the Year in 2009, and a three-time Pro Bowler.

Notes on Josh Cribbs

Years Played: 2005–2012
Position: Kick Returner/Wide Receiver
Height: 6'1"
Weight: 192
Hometown: Washington, DC
Current Residence: Cleveland, OH
Occupation: Spokesperson for the YMCA, Charity Events, and Appears on NBC Station in Cleveland, talking Browns during the season
Accomplishments: Helped lead Dunbar High School in Washington, D.C., to three consecutive DCIAA football titles and lettered in four sports: football, basketball, baseball, and swimming. In his final year at Dunbar, completed 130 of 277 passes for 2,022 yards, nine touchdowns, and five interceptions. At Kent State, played quarterback and is one of two true freshmen in NCAA history to both rush and pass for 1,000 yards. Holds numerous records at Kent State, including rushing touchdowns (38), pass completions (616), pass attempts (1,123), passing yardage (7,169), touchdowns scored (41), and points scored (246). Signed with the Browns as undrafted free agent and went on to play for ten NFL seasons, eight with Cleveland, one each with the New York Jets and the Indianapolis Colts. Tied the NFL career record with eight kickoff returns for touchdowns, and also the NFL record with two kickoffs of 100 yards or more returned for touchdowns in a single game. Lifetime average of 26.1 yards per kick return, and 10.7 yards per punt return.
Nickname: None

Josh Cribbs is still active in the Cleveland area and is a favorite with Browns fans. (Photo courtesy of Josh Cribbs)

"Fans couldn't imagine a player like me not being drafted," Cribbs said. "And I wanted people to just assume that I was drafted, because that means I did a good job.

"Because before and after every game I would look at myself in the mirror and tell myself, 'I'm gonna give it my all. Even if I mess up, I'm gonna do it going full speed.' I was able to live with myself knowing that I gave it my all every single play, every game. I didn't hold back. I wasn't the type of player to step out of bounds early on a play."

Born in June of 1983 in the Nation's Capital, Cribbs was named a first-team All-Met selection by the *Washington Post* in his senior season of 2000 at Dunbar High School, where he played quarterback.

While in high school he lettered in four sports: football, baseball, basketball, and swimming and helped Dunbar win three consecutive DCIAA football titles.

He went on to Kent State, where he again played quarterback, and to this day holds the record as the all-time offensive leader with 10,839 yards.

In 45 games during his four seasons at Kent State, Cribbs threw for 45 touchdowns and scored another 38 rushing. He is still one of just four Kent State players to have their numbers retired.

He came to the Browns as an undrafted free agent, and after a successful first season after making the team he inked a six-year contract with the franchise in 2006.

Cribbs made the Pro Bowl in 2007 and was also a first team All-Pro as a kick returner. He helped the Browns to a 10–6 mark, missing the playoffs by just one game.

The next season, Cribbs continued to make a transition more and more to wide receiver and caught 58 passes over the 2007 and 2008 seasons combined.

The team, though, didn't have much success in 2008, winning just four games, and in 2009 things got worse under coach Eric Mangini, and they started the season 1–11.

With just one win, the Browns got ready for a week 14 prime-time game on a Thursday night against the rival Pittsburgh Steelers, who had beaten the Browns earlier in the season, 27–14, in week six.

The weather would be a factor for both teams; on a cold December night the wind chill at kickoff was six below, making for a memorable night by the lakefront.

The Game

I have so many favorite games. Fans tell me what their favorite games are. It's hard for me to say which game is my favorite, but it's just the fans that put Cleveland over the top.

Beating the Steelers in 2009, we then went on a four-game win streak under Eric Mangini. It was one of the coldest games, and we beat them just doing the Wildcat.

It had been a long time since we beat the Steelers. The last time the Browns beat the Steelers prior to that game was before I got there.

That was our Super Bowl. That was our playoff game. That gave us bragging rights throughout the rest of the year.

We were on a mission. We just came off our bye week. We were riled up and we said basically we had a brand new season. You know, every season when you have a losing year you kind of wish you could go back and change things, so that bye week came at a critical time, and it was like a turning point for everybody.

The offense, the defense, and the special teams. And we were like, "Look, we have a chance to go back and change things." We say every year, and usually we would get a bye week early in the season and then at the end of the year we'll say to ourselves, "Man, we wish we could go back and play that game over."

We play every division team twice, so this was our second time facing the Steelers in 2009. We had played them already. That was our second chance.

We went into the game as if we got to start the season over, and we had already seen these guys, so we were like, "Let's go out and play like we wish we could have the first time."

It was like a do-over. Football is the biggest team sport, and when you have everybody on the same page and everybody believing, I feel like whatever team has the most players who have the same goal will win.

A lot of fans remember that. We knocked the Steelers out of play-off contention.

We knew that running the Wildcat, it was like uneven. Usually the quarterback is the extra guy, he hands it off, and then there's just enough guys to get blocks and there was always an extra guy for the runner. But by the quarterback, being me, we always had an extra guy to block their extra guy.

If everybody did their job, then it would be successful every time. We actually ran a Wildcat play on like third and 13, because there was nothing else we could do, and we got the first down.

That kind of was like the nail in the coffin, because it was late in the fourth quarter. That extended our drive. We drove down the field all day and the Steelers' game plan was, "We're not gonna let Cribbs run all over us."

Guys still joke today, like Mike Adams will say, "Yeah, it was Cribbs against the Steelers."

But I say, no, it was everybody. I couldn't have done it without my blockers. The Steelers gave us bulletin board material because they said they were going to shut the Wildcat down.

For me to be utilized in the way that I was, I felt like I was the quarterback of the game, and even though it was 20 below zero and I couldn't feel my face, I fed off the energy of the fans. Every first down the crowd rang out, giving me more energy.

I remember Joe Thomas pulling around the corner, receivers blocking down the field. Everybody was trying to spring me.

We felt that the Steelers played well as a team on defense, but we were better. We felt like they were down and out. We made sure we were going to spoil everything that they had going on, thinking that they were just going to come in and run over us. It wasn't nothing special.

All we had was the Wildcat and they knew it. And they still couldn't stop it. And we didn't care if they knew the play, they still had to stop it.

Sometimes they would bring the safety down, Troy Polamalu, and I would just cut it back. A couple times I cut it back across the field and ran for a long gain, juking people out, switching directions, and ran the opposite side when they would try to load up one side.

There was really nothing they could do to stop it. We were moving on all cylinders. Lawrence Vickers was the greatest fullback that I had. He was plowing the way. They were no match for us that game.

The defense was working. Our fans were cheering, the 12th man off the bench. You couldn't ask for a greater game, especially against the Steelers. It was like our Super Bowl.

The ground felt like cement. The cheering of the fans made it feel like plush grass. I hit the ground so hard, and Lawrence Vickers picked me up. The roar of the fans brought life into me and healed my wounds.

They always say it hurts harder when you lose; you can feel the cold even more when you're losing. It's the opposite effect when you're winning. It's not as cold.

The ground is not as hard. The pain is not as bad.

So that game it rang out for me because, you know, we're out there in spandex and basically nothing on in 20 below freezing. Literally, I can't feel my face.

We sound like we all have novicaine splashed on our lips and the roar of the fans kept us from being hurt and feeling the elements of the game.

I say that in particular because we won. I played a lot of games against the Steelers where I had success. Many of my touchdowns throughout my career came against the Steelers.

I would score touchdowns at their home. I remember the best touchdown, the "Immaculate Deception" is what they called it, it was a 100-yard touchdown, it bounced off me and kind of juked the Steelers out, and I ended up going 100 yards and scoring.

We went ahead in the game. There was eight minutes left, but we still ended up losing. And that's kind of the tale of how I had all these great games against the Steelers, but we'd always end up losing.

But that 2009 Thursday night game when it was 20 below, we won that game. The Steelers came in saying they were gonna shut us down and stop the Wildcat, and we just ran it down their throats.

That was one of the best, not just for me, but for the fans to actually have some success.

Our record was only 5–11 that year, but it didn't matter. We went to Quicken Loans Arena for a Cavs game a few days after that, and they put us up on the Jumbotron and gave us floor seats, and treated us like royalty.

We could have thrown our own parade when we beat the Steelers, and it would have been justified to the fans of the land from all over. Just because we beat the Steelers.

Traditionally, I would try to tell the new guys how important that game is. How important that rivalry is.

Any given Sunday, any team in the NFL can win because you have so many different people from so many different walks of life, some who think it's just about the contract, some who think, "I just wanna do my job." But when you get all the players playing selflessly for one another and for the success of the team, that team will be victorious.

For the last four weeks of the season that was us. We went on a four-game win streak, and the Steelers were just one of the teams in our way.

The Aftermath

After the Browns topped the Steelers on national television, Cribbs was not done with accomplishing the amazing.

The following week, he put on an all-time performance in Kanas City, returning six kickoffs for 269 yards and scoring two touchdowns.

He returned a kick 100 yards in the first quarter to make it 10–3 Browns, and then later, in the second quarter, after the Chiefs reeled off 21 straight points, he ran another kickoff back 103 yards to give the Browns a 24–20 lead in a game they eventually won, 41–34.

Cribbs made the Pro Bowl for the Browns and was a first team All-Pro, as well as the 2009 Cleveland Browns' MVP.

"For me on special teams, it was a given," Cribbs said. "That year I took my whole Special Teams unit to the Pro Bowl with me. We all played for one another. I made sure to tell them that it's not me doing this alone.

"I would make sure that when I did an interview or something, I would mention everyone by name. When I went to the Pro Bowl, I had all their jerseys with me, and every day for the Pro Bowl I would wear one of their jerseys and represent the guys that were busting their tails for me, blocking for me to get me there."

Cribbs continued to be all about "team." In 2010 he returned 20 punts and 40 kicks, and the next season caught 38 passes while returning punts and kicks, as well.

He stayed with the Browns through the 2012 season, still playing at a high level, averaging 27.4 yards returned per kick.

"I made sure it was a team effort, it wasn't just me. People would know I just was running through the holes that those guys provided," Cribbs said.

"Because I did that, anytime they would miss a block or an assignment they would run to me to say, 'Man, it was my fault. I promise I'll block for you from now on, it'll never happen again.' The accountability was far beyond a coach yelling at them.

"They held themselves accountable. Some of them were sick to their stomachs if they weren't able to get a block or messed up on a play. That's when I knew we were at a new level on that Special

Teams Unit, and it filtered down to the offense. We got started late that year, but it started to filter down throughout the whole team."

Cribbs was released in March of 2013 and felt his NFL career would continue as he inked an offseason deal with the Oakland Raiders.

A bad preseason led to Cribbs getting his release, and from there he appeared in just 12 games over the next two seasons with the New York Jets and Indianapolis Colts before walking away from the game.

Cribbs will be the first to admit his time with the Browns was by far and away the best, with a lot of the credit going to the fans.

"I have been fortunate to play in Oakland, New York, and Indianapolis, and to play in other stadiums, and be on a team that traditionally has won, but in the present day has not been able to win or be successful; our fan base has still been the best," Cribbs said.

Cribbs remains local in the Cleveland area and continues to give back to the Browns fans and community through his charitable deeds.

"I was highly involved in the community when I played, so I don't see a reason for me to not transition to the community now that I'm not with the team," Cribbs said.

"One thing I did when I was playing with the Browns was 'Shop with a Jock' at Wal-Mart during Christmas time. So I did it this past Christmas. I let them know that I'm not with the team, but I'm still going to do it. I called it Christmas Cribbs.

"I don't like the term 'Jock' because it implies that I'm not intelligent. The year of the dumb jock is over. A lot of athletes are very intelligent. I have a degree. Many of us have undergrad degrees and Master's degrees. But I'm still highly involved with the community and giving back."

CHAPTER 18

JIM PYNE

Offensive Lineman 1999–2000
The Game: October 31, 1999, vs New Orleans Saints at
Louisiana Superdome
CLEVELAND BROWNS 21—NEW ORLEANS SAINTS 16

WHEN THE CLEVELAND Browns were coming back into the league in 1999 after a three-year absence, there was great wonder as to which player they would choose first to "kick off" the franchise in the "Expansion Draft."

Players from other teams were put on a list for the Browns to choose from. Some too old, some too expensive, some just out of place and needing a fresh start.

Two months before the Browns took quarterback Tim Couch with their first overall pick, they filled some of their roster in the expansion draft, which took place February 9, 1999, in Canton, Ohio, the home of the Pro Football Hall of Fame.

One player who was on the list was then Detroit Lions offensive lineman Jim Pyne. The 28-year-old had just completed a season with the Lions in which he was playing center blocking for Hall of Fame running back Barry Sanders.

Now, he was on a list to join a new franchise in a city that was starving to get pro football back.

Pyne was on the short list of players to be brought to Canton, as the Browns and NFL wanted some players to be able to come on stage for the crowd and the viewing public to see.

Notes on Jim Pyne

Years Played: 1999-2000
Hometown: Milford, Massachusetts
Current Residence: Tampa, FL
Position: Offensive Line
Height: 6'2"
Weight: 297
Occupation: Executive Vice President at Wheels Up Luxury Jet Service
Accomplishmets: Played nine seasons in the NFL, with Tampa Bay, Detroit, Cleveland, and the Philadelphia Eagles. Was a seventh round pick, 200th overall, by Buccaneers in the 1994 NFL Draft. Father and grandfather both played professional football. Grandfather George Pyne II played for the Providence Steam Roller of the NFL in 1931. Father George Pyne III played for the Boston Patriots of the AFL in 1965. Started 38 of his 42 games with the Buccaneers between 1995 to 1997, playing left guard. Played his college ball at Virginia Tech from 1990 to 1993 and as a senior in 1993 was selected as a unanimous All-American, the first ever for a player from Virginia Tech. Was honored with the Dudley Award, which is given to the Commonwealth of Virginia's outstanding player of the year. He was a finalist for both the Lombardi Award and the Outland Trophy. Virginia Tech retired his number 73, one of only four football numbers retired by the school in over 100 years of football.
Nickname: None

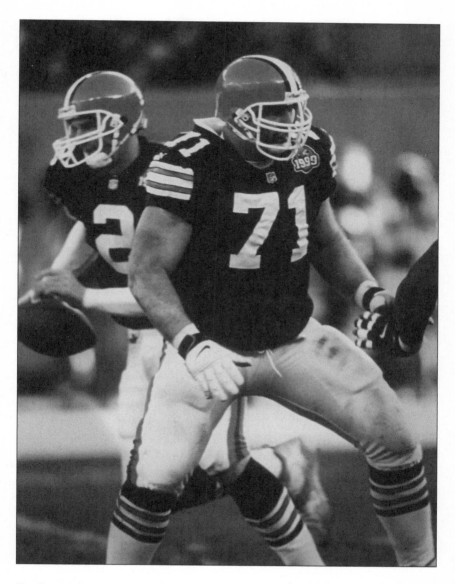

Jim Pyne gets ready to block for Tim Couch. (Photo courtesy of Jim Pyne)

"It's something I will never forget; it was an awesome feeling, a special feeling for sure. It was a special day that I will always remember. It was truly a special deal for me, and something I will never forget," Pyne said. "I remember the great people at the Browns at the time, and it was such an exciting time, you could feel it in the air, it was palpable."

There was no guarantee that Pyne would be the first pick, but he took on his normal humble attitude and soaked in the excitement that he almost for sure as a veteran lineman would end up on the Browns roster at some point in the draft.

"I was flown in the night before, and just the feeling, getting to meet Bernie Kosar, all the new coaches, Carmen Policy, Mr. Lerner, getting to go to dinner, it was just a fun, fun deal," Pyne said.

"We went to dinner down at Blue Point in Downtown Cleveland, they put us in a private room, me and some of the others that would be involved in the draft."

The following day Pyne, along with the other players invited, made their way to Canton Civic Center, where 4,000 fans sold out the event with the anticipation that it would be a new day for the Cleveland Browns.

It would also be a new day and a new start for Pyne, but little did he know he was about to become the first overall pick by the Browns in the expansion draft, and his name would forever go down in Browns history as the player to re-start their franchise.

"They kept it a secret who was going first. My agent said, 'Hey, I think they are going to take you first,' but I said, 'Well, we'll see and whatnot,' and it was interesting; the day of the draft they kept us in a back room, and then the thing started and they came and tapped me on the shoulder and said, 'Come on, Jim,' and I just said, 'OK,' and I walked through the curtains, out into that whole scene, and it was just wild.

"The place was going nuts, it was a great entry into my time into Cleveland; it was a time I will never forget."

Pyne held up a Browns jersey officially announcing the team was back, and now had a player to go along with it.

They would choose 32 players that afternoon in Canton, a number of whom never saw the roster come opening day 1999 against the rival Pittsburgh Steelers.

Pyne did see the roster, starting every game for the Browns the team's first season back in the league in 1999.

The guard was treated like royalty in Cleveland that first season, getting attention from fans when he walked down the streets in Downtown Cleveland, a treatment somewhat odd for an offensive lineman.

"I played in Tampa, then Detroit, Cleveland, and then Philadelphia, and I coached with the Bucs for two years, and coached for the Saints for one, and I tell people all the time the best place to play, live is most definitely Cleveland," Pyne said.

"When you walk through the streets of Cleveland the fans were great, they were very knowledgeable of the players, and then you had the history of the team, which was unbelievable."

While that 1999 team wasn't very good, winning just two games, they were both memorable. One was an upset win in Pittsburgh after they were dominated by the Steelers, 43–0, in their first game.

The other win was one that no one could have scripted, a game against Mike Ditka and the New Orleans Saints on Halloween in New Orleans.

A game which, to this day, provided one of the more memorable endings in Browns history.

The Game

The first year wasn't a great year, but the game that I remember the most was our first win, October 31, 1999, down in New Orleans.

We had a three-game road trip; it was our last game on the road before we came home for Baltimore. Two weeks later we went on to beat the Pittsburgh Steelers; we kind of got on a roll there a little bit.

We lost a lot of close games, we had a ton of injuries. We were a new team and we just had no depth. We started to get some injuries and then losing close games, a thin team, a very young team was really hard.

They weren't all that good of a team, and we went down there feeling confident going in, like we had a good chance at a win, and things went well.

I just had a feeling we were finally going to win one of these, and something good was going to happen here soon.

We lost to the Bengals at home, 18–17, a few weeks earlier, and 19–7 to the Patriots, 17–10 to the Ravens, so we were in a lot of games, and they were close. Even the last game of the year we lost to the Colts by a point, and they were a playoff team.

It was time to win a game, it was a fun thing, and the way it happened for us made it more exciting.

We needed to win some close games for the season to go better than it did, but that first game was special, and then that first win at New Orleans was special.

Mike Ditka was the coach at the time for the Saints, and I remember we were trailing and it was the last play of the game; it was a "Sprint right."

Tim Couch, our quarterback at the time, rolled to the right. I was on the left side of Tim, Dave Wohlabaugh was the center, I was the guard, and Lomas Brown was the tackle.

We just had to kind of stand back and protect the left side, and then Tim rolled out, heaved the ball up there deep, and Kevin Johnson caught it, and we won the game, 21–16.

For those of us that had been there from the beginning, like myself, went through the draft, it was like nothing you had ever done before.

We were all new to Cleveland, we had a new staff, young players, old players, this and that. We played five preseason games, and then we had 16 games in a row, we had no bye week.

Everyone looked at us like, "Well, we have the Cleveland Browns this week, we'll beat them up." It was a tough deal, tough season, but something we were all proud of.

I was named captain at the end of the year; that was special to me, being the first pick and then getting that honor.

I've been on great teams, and it's easier to be a captain on a great team when you're winning and everyone is doing well, but when you're at the lowest low, and guys look at you as a leader, that's when character is revealed.

It's kind of the story of my life: when things go bad I can kind of stay strong and gather the troops.

That first win, that last play, it was kind of symbolic of the fight we had that season. I remember running down the field after Kevin caught the pass and there was a huge pile, and I remember it seemed like the whole organization jumped on Kevin and Tim.

I remember throwing the coaches on top of the pile. We all needed a feel-good something, and that was it, Halloween night in New Orleans, it was a special deal.

They kicked a field goal that put them up, 16–14, with 21 seconds left, and I remember going into the huddle and I remember saying, "We can do this, this stuff happens."

I'm not taking credit for what happened, but you have to believe you can do it, and it was weird, probably because of the way it worked out. I had a feeling this thing wasn't over, but who could have predicted that?

I had never been part of something like that in all my years of football where literally we had just 21 seconds left and then it comes down to the last pass, you're throwing it to win the game or lose the game, and it was just an awesome feeling in the fact it was our first victory.

I remember looking over at Ditka and he's a pretty animated guy, and he's lying on the sidelines, he looked like he was dead, and I'm sure he's probably thinking, "Holy cow, we just lost to the Cleveland Browns, who were winless."

The Aftermath

The jubilant win over the Saints was followed by an awful loss at home to the Ravens, a 41–9 defeat that seemed to deflate the team following the big win.

The next week after the Ravens game, the Browns pulled off their most satisfying game of the year, a win over the hated Steelers in Pittsburgh, 16–15, when Phil Dawson kicked a field goal on the final play of the game.

It was to be the last win that year for the Browns, who ended the season at 2–14. For Pyne, though, he was having the time of his life, enjoying the fan base and culture in Cleveland.

"I had a radio show, a kids' TV show, I really had it going on in Cleveland, and I was playing well, as good as I had at any point in my career. The unfortunate thing is, in that second year I tore my ACL," Pyne said.

"Then they fired Chris Palmer and brought in Butch Davis, and I was an older guy making some money. I wasn't his guy; he wanted to get rid of older guys. He wanted to restructure my contract and I said, 'Okay, just guarantee me the league minimum,' and he wouldn't do it."

Pyne and his agent had a choice to make when it came to staying with the Browns or asking out. He knew he wanted his NFL career to continue, but with Davis the writing was clearly on the wall.

"My agent felt that this guy wasn't the guy and that I didn't want to be there. I ended up in Philadelphia, went to the NFC Championship, so I had a better experience there. It's sad how it ended for me, the knee injury kind of ended my career," Pyne said.

The knee injury was tough for Pyne to swallow, but he knows that looking back he simply wasn't the type of player he was during the prime of his career.

"Looking back, I was never the same player after I hurt my knee. I wasn't the same from a movement standpoint.

"A guy like John Elway, he was able to walk away after winning a Super Bowl, but for most of us it doesn't end the way you want it to end. I'm glad I could move on with my life, I am healthy now."

Pyne now is Executive Vice President at Wheels Up, a luxury jet service in Tampa, Florida, that provides a service to those who need to rent or use a luxury plane.

He was ready to make the transition after the NFL and has done so very well, working hard and making a life away from the game he played from ages 24 to 30.

"I knew there would be life after football and I prepared for that," Pyne said. "Football doesn't define me. I learned a lot of great lessons and met a lot of great people, but I knew when it was over I had to get up and work, and I work every day."

As for his memories of his time with the Browns, he said that looking back at his NFL career, being the first pick in the expansion draft, and playing two seasons in Cleveland, there was nothing quite like it.

"I was on some really good teams, but by far the best time I had as a player in pro football being in the community was in Cleveland, and it's because of the fans," Pyne said.

"It's an amazing place, amazing people, the facility was beautiful, we had great ownership. Now that I am away from it, it's sad to see they haven't pulled it together as an organization. So many people have come and gone out of there, they just haven't had the right mix.

"Something is off, and that's sad to see, because those are the best fans I have ever seen. I live in Tampa now, but in Cleveland football is a way of life. You work hard all week and go to the stadium on Sunday."

CHAPTER 19

BRIAN HANSEN

Punter 1991–1993

The Game: October 13, 1991, vs Washington Redskins at RFK Stadium

WASHINGTON REDSKINS 42—CLEVELAND BROWNS 17

IT STARTED WITH a fun outdoor game played with his older brothers. By the time it was said and done, it led to a 15-year career punting in the NFL.

That's just part of the story for former Cleveland Browns punter Brian Hansen, who played for the Browns from 1991 to 1993.

He was there for the start of the Bill Belichick era in Cleveland and got to see the coach who went on to eventually rack up four Super Bowl titles with the New England Patriots begin his head coaching career.

"Bill was an X's and O's guy," Hansen recalls. "It was kind of hard to figure out what he was thinking. He was always thinking; he's a tough guy to get to know and try to figure out.

"He was not a real 'players' coach,' if you will. I'm sure he's mellowed a little bit, but he had very high expectations, talking about focusing."

Hansen was born in October of 1960 in Hawarden, Iowa, and his earliest tries at punting a football started while participating in punt, pass, and kick competitions as a youngster.

He and his brothers developed a game that helped him practice his kicking skills, using his backyard with a couple of trees as a playing field.

Notes on Brian Hansen

Years Played: 1991-1993
Position: Punter
Height: 6'4"
Weight: 215
Hometown: Hawarden, IA
Current Residence: Sioux Falls, IA
Occupation: Ministry Coordinator for the Fellowship of Christian Athletes in South Dakota
Accomplishments: Played his high school ball at West Sioux High School, where he started playing various positions, and then in his junior year didn't play and instead was a pole vaulter. He returned to football for his senior season, and was a tight end as well as punter. Went to college at Sioux Falls College and was a second-team All-American his junior year, and in his senior year was first-team All-American, focusing more and more on punting. Was drafted by the New Orleans Saints in the ninth round of the 1984 Draft, the 237th overall pick. Played for five seasons with the Saints and was a Pro Bowl punter his rookie season, punting 69 times for an average of 43.8 yards per punt. Moved to the Patriots after taking off the 1989 season due to injury and then moved to Cleveland for three seasons, averaging 42.8 yards per punt. Went to the Jets to start the 1994 season and played there for five years, averaging 42.4 yards per punt. Also threw three passes in his NFL career for 45 yards and a touchdown. During his NFL career, punted 1,057 times with an average of 42.3 yards per kick.
Nickname: None

Browns punter Brian Hansen kicks during a game at Cleveland Stadium. (Photo courtesy of Brian Hansen)

"We had two sets of poplar trees," Hansen said. "We played a game called 'kickback,' and you would kick the ball from wherever you caught it, starting at a certain point, and the idea was to kick it into the trees, and you would get a point for that."

"That was one of the many games I played in the backyard with my brothers. I got to a point where I kicked it into the trees to over the trees; that's where my hang time came from."

In high school at West Sioux, Hansen started playing different positions his freshman and sophomore seasons, and then didn't play at all his junior year.

He instead became a pole vaulter, and it wasn't until a trip to see a college game between the University of South Dakota and North Dakota State that he got the kicking bug in him again. Watching two of the best punters go back and forth got the juices flowing for him to again go out for football.

His senior year, Hansen was the starting tight end and also the punter, and continued to work on his punting more and more.

"I kicked my leg off, and got a whopping $500 scholarship to Sioux Falls College," Hansen said.

In college he was not only a punter, but also played tight end and wide receiver. He was a second-team All-American his junior year, and in his senior year was first-team All-American.

He did suffer an injury that forced him even more to focus on punting when a player ran into him on a punt and he blew out his knee, but returned two weeks later.

At that point he wasn't able to play wide out or tight end and had to place all his focus on his punting.

"It allowed me to prepare to do what I was supposed to do. It allowed me to focus, so it worked out well," Hansen said. "There's something about the challenge of being a kicker, I sort of gravitated toward that."

He entered the 1984 NFL Draft but was really preparing to end up as an undrafted free agent. To his surprise, he was picked in the draft by the New Orleans Saints.

"I didn't have the real expectations of being drafted," Hansen said. "I had met with the Cowboys the night before the draft; they wanted to sign me as a free agent if I didn't get drafted. I was excited about that. Then the Saints took me in the ninth round."

Not having felt that he would be drafted, Hansen didn't exactly have all kinds of thoughts about what it would be like when his name was finally called, or even getting a call from a team.

He still was able to embrace the moment and took it all in stride when the Saints came marching into his life in the ninth round of the 1984 draft.

"I remember hearing, growing up, all these stories about local guys getting drafted, and expectations, and how excited they were," Hansen said. "I just didn't expect to get drafted, but it was kind of a neat deal."

Hansen made a solid impact with the Saints right away. During the 1984 season he punted 63 times, putting up a very good rookie average of 43.8, good enough to get to the Pro Bowl.

After five good seasons with the Saints, Hansen had to undergo surgery on his kicking foot; he had torn all the ligaments in his right ankle and wasn't sure he would play again.

The somewhat new procedure ended up as a success, and he was ready to play again after missing the 1989 season.

He inked a deal with the New England Patriots in 1990, a year that saw the Patriots win just one game under coach Rud Rust, going 1–15.

Hansen then signed with the Browns, who were undergoing a new look with a new regime, as Bill Belichick was set to enter his first year as head coach for the team.

"They had a brand new facility the first year; I had never seen anything like that before. I kind of felt like I was in the big leagues."

The job wasn't Hansen's right away. He had to battle a couple of other players in order to win the punting position in camp.

"We had three guys competing for the job, an all-out battle for the position, and Bill told me I was his guy, and I was there for three years," Hansen said.

Hansen and the Browns improved right away. The team won six games that first season, after winning just three games in 1990.

They sat at 2–3 as they prepared for a huge test for this young team in week seven against the Washington Redskins, a club that was in the midst of a Super Bowl run.

The Game

The thing with punters is, we don't have a whole lot of highlights.

We played the Washington Redskins in D.C. It was the 1991 season and they were undefeated, and to that point had three shutouts at home in beating the Lions, Cardinals, and Eagles.

They ended up with the Super Bowl that year; they beat Buffalo in the Super Bowl.

So we're playing them and they have this streak going, and sure enough we score on this kind of freak play, a sneak play; it was a fake field goal.

It was one of Belichick's bag of tricks that you always have to be aware of.

As far as the deception part of it, you have to be within the hash-marks at a certain point.

Webster Slaughter, who caught the touchdown, kind of went off like he was having equipment problems, and he was kind of running off the field.

We were lined up in field goal formation, and he was telling the coaches, "Hey, my chin strap is messed," or something like that, and then he just stepped up to the sideline and got set.

Once I saw he was set and uncovered, I had the green light to run the fake field goal. It actually worked.

I lobbed it over to the end zone, he caught it, and it was a touchdown.

I went to the sideline and caught a lot of slack from Bernie (Kosar) and Vinny (Testaverde), saying that I had thrown a duck.

I told them I had a guy in my face, and Bernie says, "You don't know what having a guy in your face is," which I laughed with him about.

As far as the play went, we always practiced something every week with Bill, something that he would see with a team's tendencies and weaknesses, and what personnel they would play against us.

They would always come up with something, a gadget play or something during that week. Very seldom would you use it, but every once in a while they would give you the green light.

It was really on me to make the call if I saw he was open, and we scored the first touchdown on them, but we didn't win the game.

It was one of my claims to fame I guess, throwing a touchdown pass. I was what Belichick referred to as the "disaster quarterback."

Belichick had heard that I played quarterback I don't know if it was because maybe I looked like a quarterback at 6-foot-4, but for some reason he thought I could play quarterback, or fill that role.

I sat in during a couple weeks of training camp with the quarterbacks, learning the offense, which was way beyond me, so they ended up giving me six plays.

Four of which were running plays, and two short passing plays. That was part of my offensive arsenal. So I was the "disaster quarterback" for Belichick and Pete Carroll.

I was 3-for-3 in my career, no picks, a touchdown; my quarterback rating was pretty high.

The Aftermath

The year 1991 was a turning point for the Browns; they started to show signs of buying into what Belichick was selling them.

Even with that, Hansen didn't really think Belichick would become the legendary future Hall of Fame coach that he's become today with the Patriots.

"I didn't see the potential greatness in what Bill was doing, I felt like there wasn't that intangible that you need as a coach to get your players to play for you," Hansen remembers.

"I did not see that magic going on there, where you would say that this is going to be the next greatest coach in the NFL.

"I've seen specials where they had this great staff in Cleveland, and many said it was the system, and that if they would have stayed the team would have been a winner; I just didn't see that."

Hansen lasted three seasons with the Browns, and in those three years he averaged 42.8 yards per punt, the highest of any average of any team he played with in his career.

From the Browns, Hansen moved on to the New York Jets, where he punted for five seasons, from 1994 to 1998, and wrapped up his career with two games in Washington with the Redskins in 1999.

"In hindsight, looking back, I was blessed to have the opportunity to be around that long," Hansen said. "I didn't expect to be in the league that long.

"To stick around that long and look at the circumstances and situations, and exist that long, it's sometimes hard to believe."

Now working as part of the Fellowship of Christian Athletes in South Dakota, Hansen still looks back to his days in Cleveland as some of his favorites over a long punting career.

"It was a pleasant surprise. I didn't know much about Cleveland," Hansen recalls. "Of the places I played, it was probably the most memorable stay, being there three years."

He recalls the city as well as Old Cleveland Stadium, a place that was filled with plenty of memories before it was dismantled after the team moved to Baltimore following the 1995 season, and a new stadium stands in its place to this day. "It was a great city to play in, in terms of their love for the Browns," Hansen said. "Playing in the old stadium, it wasn't a kicker's or punter's favorite place to play, but there was something unique and special about it."

CHAPTER 20

ORPHEUS ROYE

Defensive End/Tackle 2000–2007
The Game: January 5, 2003, vs Pittsburgh Steelers at Heinz Field
PITTSBURGH STEELERS 36—CLEVELAND BROWNS 33

S INCE THE CLEVELAND Browns re-entered the NFL as a franchise in 1999, the team has continually gone out nearly every season and signed free agents.

Like most NFL teams, the Browns are always hopeful that these free agents will bring with them the experience and success they have had with other franchises.

One free agent who came to the Browns and had a very successful run for eight seasons was defensive lineman Orpheus Roye.

Roye came to Cleveland following the 1999 season from a franchise that the Browns know all too well: their biggest rival, the Pittsburgh Steelers.

For the former sixth-round pick by the Steelers, it wasn't exactly an easy adjustment going to a team that was still trying to find itself after just returning to the league one year earlier.

"It was challenging. Very challenging," Roye recalls.

"Coming from Pittsburgh, it was a franchise that was pretty much established for many years, and had a history of Super Bowls and a tradition that they carried.

"The structure of it was very different from Cleveland. When I got to Cleveland it was a whole new regime. It was different to go from

Notes on Orpheus Roye

Years Played: 2000-2007
Position: Defensive End/Tackle
Height: 6'4"
Weight: 320
Hometown: Miami, FL
Current Residence: Atlanta, GA
Occupation: Operations Manager at Jewel of the South Construction in Atlanta
Accomplishments: From Miami, was a star player at Miami Springs High School before moving on to Florida State. Was part of a Seminoles team that won three Orange Bowls and a Sugar Bowl, and every year finished in the top five in the polls. Moved to the Steelers after being the 200th draft pick in the 1996 NFL Draft, taken in the sixth round. Played mostly special teams, and then started nine games in 1998, and all 16 for Pittsburgh in 1999. Was signed by the Browns in the offseason and came to the team with a six-year deal. Started 16 games in 2000 and 2002, and 15 games in 2003. Played eight years total in Cleveland, starting 102 of 113 games, totaling 284 tackles, 99 assists, and one safety. Played six games with the Steelers in 2008, a season that ended with a Super Bowl win over the Arizona Cardinals in Super Bowl XLIII.
Nickname: None

Browns DL Orpheus Roye played on both sides of the Browns-Steelers rivalry, winning a Super Bowl ring with Pittsburgh in 2008. (Photo courtesy of Orpheus Roye)

only having one losing season, where we were in the playoffs pretty much every year, to going to Cleveland to an organization that was trying to get back in the swing of things, and trying to get back to being recognized as a competitive team.

"There were definitely growing pains."

Roye, born in 1973, was raised in Miami and underwent a number of hardships growing up. His father, who was barely around, passed away when Roye was just nine.

Before he was born, his family lost a son who would have been Roye's older brother, and then when he was 13 he lost his two-year-old sister tragically in a house fire.

Roye turned to football as an outlet to, hopefully, one day help his family and ended up being a star player at Miami Springs High School.

He went on to star at Florida State, playing on a defensive line that saw his teams rank in the top five each year of his four seasons there, winning the Orange Bowl three times, and the Sugar Bowl once.

He was chosen by the Steelers in the sixth round, 200th overall pick, in the 1996 NFL Draft. He was going to a team a year following Pittsburgh's Super Bowl appearance, so playing time with the Steelers at first would be hard to come by.

Roye continued to work hard and was a key member of the Steelers' special teams for most of his first two seasons.

When he did get the chance to play on the line, he made the most of it. He started one game in 1996 and had a fumble recovery.

In 1997, the Steelers reached the AFC Championship Game and he got another start, helping the Steelers shut down the Bengals in a 20–3 win on November 16th, in which he recorded a sack. By 1998, he was getting more and more looks on the line, starting nine games, before finally, in 1999, starting all 16 for the Steelers.

That 1999 season saw him pick off a pass, force and recover a fumble, and register 4.5 sacks. In one game against the Bengals, he even batted down three passes against first-round pick Akili Smith.

After that season, the Steelers had a tough decision to make with the fourth-year pro: either make him a big free agency offer or let him walk.

Roye wasn't exactly sure what to expect in free agency but was in for a shock when the Browns came calling, offering him a whopping deal: six years at $30 million, with a $7.5 million dollar signing bonus.

The money was enough to take care of his family and also set him up to be a key component for the Browns' defense for a number of years to come.

"It was a great experience. One that really caught me off guard," Roye said of being a free agent.

"At the time I never really wanted to leave Pittsburgh, but my agent said, 'Cleveland really wants you,' and they were going to 'pursue me very hard.'

"I heard him, but I really wasn't listening, and then when they came with the offer I was like 'Oh!' They were offering me more than Pittsburgh. So I kind of went with the money, and the rest was history."

Roye was placed immediately into the Browns' defensive starting lineup under head coach Chris Palmer and defensive coordinator Romeo Crennel.

He was originally brought in to play left defensive end but was moved just before training camp to left tackle, a new position; but, as usual with Roye, he had no qualms about the position change.

Roye started 42 games his first three seasons with the Browns, even as the team underwent a coaching change after his first season.

Butch Davis came in to take over, and the expectations for the team were even higher, as they went 7–9 in 2001, at one point sitting at 6–4 before losing five of their last six games.

In 2002, the team again was competitive, and they found themselves in a late-season run in a position to make the postseason for the first time since 1994.

The club won its final game of the season, a memorable 24–16 win at Browns Stadium that many fans still recall as their favorite Browns game of the new regime, which had started in 1999.

The win set up a wild-card matchup with their biggest rival, Roye's old team, the Steelers, on January 5, 2003, at Heinz Field.

It was a game that didn't resemble many from the history of the rivalry—more of a throwback to an AFL game than a normal Browns-Steelers down and dirty affair.

It was also a game that Roye would never forget.

The Game

All my best games were when we played Pittsburgh. Every year my stats would get better, and the next year they'd get better than the year before.

It was something about Pittsburgh that just brought that extra motivation out of me.

The 2002 playoff game we played in January was a really good game. That was the one they came back and won, 36–33, after we had a big lead.

It was a good game. We went back and forth. It kind of showed we were back on the rise a little bit. We got the lead. We were in a good position, but then after halftime something happened, and they came back and won the game, but it still was a good game.

Just the atmosphere and for us to be up on them, and the challenge they brought, it brought the best out of us.

Even though they won, it was just an amazing game to play in. It's hard to pick just one game, but all the best games were in Pittsburgh.

We built a 24–7 lead at one point, and I definitely remember we kind of went into a different mode on defense.

It was like 3-on-6, and I kept telling the defensive line coach, "We need help. It's 2-on-1."

Their quarterback, Tommy Maddox, had all day to throw the ball, and he had a huge year, and we knew we had to stop them.

We were bringing extra DBs to try to cover, but we needed extra manpower to try to pressure the quarterback.

He could be a challenging quarterback if he had time. He didn't handle pressure very well, and that's what we didn't do.

We didn't pressure him. We were more concerned about giving up the big play at the time, but he was known for not handling pressure very well.

Other games we saw him when he was under pressure, he didn't perform as well. So all week we had a bunch of different pressures planned out that we never got to use because we jumped on them so fast that we never got to use them.

Once we had that lead we went into the prevent because we were so concerned about giving up the big plays. But what we were trying to prevent, we gave up.

We had a three-man rush, and they had five linemen plus a tight end staying in to help, so we couldn't get a pass rush; we were just standing at the line.

We stopped their run game, which is what kept giving us the momentum, and kept giving us the ball back so we could score quick.

It was funny, having played there I knew what their mentality was all about. It was like we never changed what we did. We would always say, "They have to stop us. We're not going to change what we do."

It seemed like with the Browns in that playoff game, we changed our front. Like everything we prepared for the whole week for that game, we ended up doing something totally different.

Tim Couch the week before broke his leg, and Kelly Holcomb got the chance to start the playoff game in Pittsburgh. He was in a zone, man.

All week we had a good week of practice. Things were just flowing and we felt good going into the game. So when that happened and Holcomb played that great, we kind of were not surprised because the preparation was so good that week.

When it was happening it was pretty much like what we expected to happen. But in the second half it wasn't what we expected to happen because we thought that we were gonna unleash the packages that we had, bring the pressure, but it went a whole different way.

It was like we drew on a cardboard like, "OK, this is what we're gonna do." And that's why some guys were confused, because some guys were doing things that we didn't practice.

Some guys were being left on an island. It was like a whole different second half.

And when our defensive coordinator, Foge Fazio, threw his hands up and looked around like he didn't know what to do, you kind of knew that we were in trouble.

We still had the lead late, and things just really turned when Dennis Northcutt couldn't pull in a late third-down pass.

If he would have got that first down, we would have been able to run the clock out, but since he didn't get that first down, we had to punt.

That seemed to be when the momentum changed. We were driving, and if we would have got that first down we would have put the nail in the coffin.

Instead, they got the ball back, we couldn't pressure Maddox, and he led them downfield and they scored to win the game.

The Aftermath

The loss to the Steelers was deflating. The team had leads of 24–7 and 33–21, but with Maddox throwing the ball for 367 yards and three touchdowns, the Browns couldn't hold the lead.

The team was expected to be on the rise entering the 2003 season, but instead lost eight of their last ten games and ended the season with a record of 5–11.

The 2003 campaign went downhill quickly after Davis made the decision to start Holcomb at quarterback over Couch after he threw for 429 yards and three scores in the playoff loss.

It seemed the team was divided, and there was no recovery after a 3–3 start; the club simply didn't have the same momentum carried over from the season before.

For Roye, he stayed with the Browns until after the 2007 season and had a productive career in Cleveland.

He started 102 of 113 games for the Browns during his time with the franchise, recording 284 tackles, 9.5 sacks, and a pair of interceptions.

Roye actually went back to the Steelers in 2008 and played in six games for Pittsburgh, who went on to win Super Bowl XLIII that season, beating Arizona in Tampa, Florida, 27–23.

He is one of the rare people who played for just two franchises, starting and ending his career with the Steelers, but in between playing eight seasons for Cleveland.

"Both have good fan bases," Roye said of the Steelers and Browns fans.

"I think Pittsburgh had a little bit greater of a fan base, because sometimes we would go play teams and we'd have more fans there than the home team.

"But Cleveland fans, like home games, they sell out and they're supportive. It could be raining. It could be almost below zero and they're there strong, cheering, even if we weren't winning. The fans were heavy supporters."

CHAPTER 21

TOMMY VARDELL

Running Back 1992–1995
The Game: September 14, 1992, vs Miami Dolphins at Cleveland Stadium
MIAMI DOLPHINS 27—CLEVELAND BROWNS 23

TOMMY VARDELL CAME to the Cleveland Browns as a first-round draft choice in 1992, a bruising running back from Stanford joining a crowded backfield of veterans.

It wasn't easy for Vardell to come to a team that already had a couple of established running backs, so he knew early on that he was going to have to work hard to prove he belonged.

"The day after draft day I realized that adding another running back to the roster was not what the Browns fans wanted," Vardell said. I think the headline said, "Fullback: full backfield!!"

Vardell wasn't the one to blame for the position he was put in with the Browns and has over the years felt both the positive and negative from those in Cleveland.

"I have received a number of letters over time from people in Cleveland that have told me how they respected the way that I played and how I represented myself and the values of the city when I was there," Vardell said.

"I appreciate that more than one could ever imagine. Being loved in Cleveland is probably the pinnacle of every athlete's dream in any sport. Not being liked or appreciated is probably the worst nightmare one could ever envision."

Notes on Tommy Vardell

Years Played: 1992-1995
Position: Running Back
Height: 6'2"
Weight: 234
Hometown: El Cajon, CA
Current Residence: Danville, CA
Occupation: Co-Founder of Northgate Capital, a Private Equity Investment Firm
Accomplishments: Earned his B.S. degree in Industrial Engineering from Stanford University. At Stanford, he was an Academic All-American and was honored as the top male scholar-athlete in the nation (GTE Academic All-American of the Year). Carried the ball 418 times all told at Stanford, no fumbles lost. Was given the nickname "Touchdown Tommy" by then Stanford head coach Denny Green. Was a 2009 inductee into the Stanford Athletics Hall of Fame. Played in the NFL for eight seasons, two with the Browns, two with the 49ers, and two with the Lions. Was the Browns' first-round pick in 1992, the ninth pick overall. Biggest game as a pro came in week three of 1993 when he rushed for 104 yards on 14 carries and had two catches for 22 yards in a 19–16 win over the Raiders. In his career, rushed for 1,427 yards and 18 touchdowns, with 119 catches for 1,010 yards and three scores. Nominated by Stanford for the 2017 NCAA Silver Anniversary Award.
Nickname: Touchdown Tommy

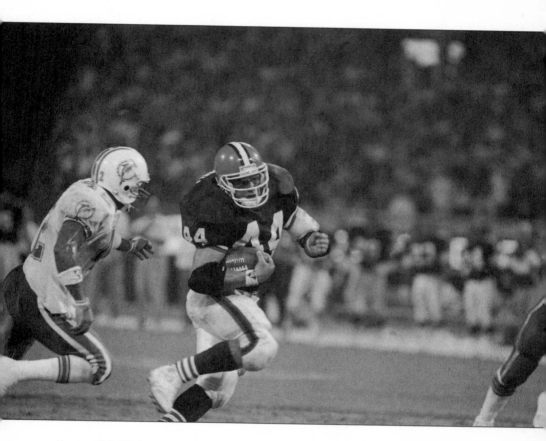

Browns RB/FB Tommy Vardell was the team's first-round pick, 9th overall, in the 1992 NFL Draft. (Photo courtesy of Tommy Vardell)

Vardell was born in El Cajon, California, the son of Ken Vardell, who was a guard at Colorado from 1959 to '61 and also was a special agent for the FBI. His mother, Travis, was a fashion model.

He started to play football at the age of eight and took to running with the football right away. In high school at El Cajon's Granite Hills High, his brother Teddy was his lead blocker, earning the nickname "Tailgatin" Teddy.

Vardell enrolled at Stanford University after high school, playing for former Minnesota Vikings and Arizona Cardinals coach Dennis Green.

He was a special type of player, and his running style was compared to the likes of Hall of Famers John Riggins and Larry Csonka.

It took some time for people to recognize Vardell for what he could do as a fullback, since he had to wait his turn to get a chance to shine, which didn't truly take place until his final season.

"I was a more natural fullback but was thrust into a running role my senior year after Glyn Milburn, the Stanford Heisman candidate, was injured," Vardell said.

Once Vardell got the chance to be the feature back, he seized it. He went on to set six Stanford records, including the single-season mark of 1,084 yards on the ground, and a school record 20 touchdowns.

One of his most memorable games was the one in which he earned his nickname "Touchdown," a game in South Bend against Notre Dame, when he crossed the goal line four times and was given the nickname by Green, his coach at the time.

Overall, Vardell ranks second in Stanford's TD history, and third in rushing. He set Stanford records for most points in a season (120), most rushing TDs in a career (37), and most carries in a game (39).

In his final season at Stanford in 1991, he was named the GTE All-Academic All-American Player of the Year as a senior, and All-Pac-10 Academic.

Not only that, he received the Pop Warner Trophy for 1991, which is presented to the Top Senior Player on the West Coast.

He was also Aloha Bowl Most Valuable Player, after he scored two touchdowns while gaining 104 yards, even though he left the game in the second half with a broken collarbone.

His draft stock went through the roof during the offseason after his 1991 campaign, and teams from all over were looking at Vardell as an option for the run game.

"I think what pushed me to a top 10 pick was my performance testing, evaluations, pro days, and team interviews. I think the football executives were looking for a certain mindset and approach to the game which was similar to my own."

It was at the combine where scouts and teams really started to take notice of just how good Vardell could be.

He ran a 4.48 in the 40, had a 38.5 inch vertical, and bench-pressed 225 pounds a whopping 24 times, something he did 32 times while in Detroit.

"This was the combination of explosiveness and speed that (Browns coach Bill) Belichick drafted," Vardell said. "But this was also hard to reconstruct after my knee injury."

"I knew the Browns and others in the top 15 were actively looking. I was thrilled when I was drafted."

Vardell was excited about coming to Cleveland to play for the Browns, a franchise steeped in history with a rabid fan base.

"I think the fans wanted an O lineman to protect (quarterback) Bernie (Kosar)," Vardell said.

"But when I got to Cleveland, I was greeted by an older gentleman who was working at the airport. He said, "Mr. Touchdown . . . so happy to have you here in Cleveland," with a warm smile and kind eyes that I still can see today.

"At that point, I realized that I was in good hands with the fans of Cleveland. Good people. Good values. I was going to be OK."

It didn't take all that long for Vardell to understand the pecking order in Cleveland, and early on he saw just how tough it was going to be to get substantial playing time in the Browns' offense behind some veteran backs.

"I realized quickly that managing playing time was going to be an issue," Vardell said.

"I would join Leroy Hoard, Kevin Mack, Eric Metcalf, and later, Ernest Byner, in the backfield.

"This was the advent of the running back by committee system. In my four years in Cleveland I think I got more than 12 carries in a game three to four times, and then I got hurt; it was a tough situation."

The rookie season for Vardell got off to a tough start with a 14–3 loss in Indianapolis to the Colts, a game that saw Vardell rush the ball nine times for 28 yards and make three catches for 36 yards.

The team was headed home for a week-two matchup with the Miami Dolphins, and while it was special for being the first home game for Vardell, it had even more flair being in prime time on *Monday Night Football.*

The Game

One of the games that I remember most was my very first home game in Cleveland against Dan Marino's Miami Dolphins.

It was my first taste of the Cleveland fans, and it also happened to be *Monday Night Football.*

Duh Duh Duh Daaahhhhhhhhh!!!!!!

I was so incredibly excited, and terrified at the same time.

I was just starting to get comfortable with the offense, and I had to protect Bernie from Bryan Cox, a 6-foot-4 linebacker that had 14 sacks that year and was an All-Pro. (The last outside linebacker I had blocked was an engineering major from Berkeley, to give some perspective).

Aside from the pass protection responsibilities, Coach Belichick installed an offense that would put Leroy, Eric, and me together in the backfield all at once.

I don't know why we didn't do that again. Seemed like it was working that game.

In preparation for the game I struggled to find my steady, confident ground. *Monday Night Football*, Cleveland Stadium, what if, what if, what if?!!!

I was too conscientious to just let go and let be. I wish I was the type that could. I always envied the guys that could stay up until 2 a.m. before a game, not study the playbook, and go out and perform like a champion the next day.

I wasn't that type.

I had to review, rehearse, and replay all of the possible scenarios in my head.

I started thinking about the city and the Browns fans, and all of the families across the nation that were gathering together to enjoy the game.

I put down the playbook and started to immerse myself in the fervor of the city in anticipation of this game, and the concern, stress, etc., melted away.

I had still not experienced a full Browns stadium yet (preseason doesn't count). When the announcer introduced our team and I ran out onto the field, I was met with a tidal wave of roar that echoed into my sternum so hard that I felt like a train was running through the stadium.

So this is Cleveland!!! Whoa, I will never forget that first introduction to a full Cleveland stadium. This was going to be a good night.

I remember the game itself like I played it a few nights ago. It wasn't my very best game statistically, and we actually lost. But the memories are incredibly distinct.

This was a game that Bernie Kosar played heroically. On a broken ankle he brought us back from a 20–3 deficit in the fourth quarter, and had us in the lead after David Brandon stripped the ball and scored on a 32-yard fumble return for a TD, and our tight end Mark Bavaro caught a short touchdown.

No one, of course, knew that Bernie had broken his ankle. He just was hobbling around, and as a rookie I wasn't totally sure what was the Bernie style and what was the injury.

At the peak of loudness and celebration, with seconds to go and despite Bernie's (and the team's) heroic efforts, Dan Marino drove down to win the game for the Dolphins.

The emotional swings in the game were so incredibly intense. Violent collisions, lead changes, *Monday Night Football*, diving catches, Hall of Fame players.

A game (seemingly) won on the battlefield echoing with the continuous roar of the Cleveland faithful, and then lost into silence as Dan Marino achieved just one more of his comeback victories.

Sometimes distinctly memorable games are also laced with some not so wonderful moments (which help with making them memorable).

On a play in the second quarter, I received what would be the hardest hit of my NFL career. I got BLASTED by John Offerdahl, the other Dolphin All-Pro linebacker.

I caught a ball over the middle with my eye on another All-Pro safety, Louis Oliver.

When I broke away from Oliver I broke into Offerdahl, who had about a 15-yard run at me.

All 250 pounds of him. My entire right side was numb. I popped up like I felt nothing. It was a little difficult to get in my stance the next play. Thank goodness I didn't have to catch the ball again until later in the game.

This was also a night that, on a 12-yard run, I came inches from scoring my first NFL touchdown. I am not sure what the ruling on the field would have been with instant replay, but I thought I was in.

But, it was not to be. This would happen again in Cincinnati a few weeks later. Sheesh. Oh, how I wish I would have scored a touchdown my rookie year!! Life would have been SOOO much easier.

But most was good. I was able to fend off Bryan Cox from getting to Bernie by tactfully placing the crown of my helmet underneath his chin when we collided.

And I ended up with 84 yards on 16 carries (5.25 yards per carry), and two catches for 29 yards, and a number of key blocks and critical first downs.

The game solidified an active role for me in the Cleveland offense.

And I was experiencing Cleveland at its finest. This was a sign of things to come. It was a launching point for me in Cleveland!

The Aftermath

Vardell's second NFL game saw him become the featured back that evening for the Browns, as he had 16 of the 24 rushes for the team against the Dolphins.

The following week, though, things were dramatically different. Vardell was not able to be as impactful in the offense, as the Browns won their first game of the year, beating the Raiders, 28–16.

"The next game we played the Raiders in Los Angeles, and I had six short-yardage carries and was a lead blocker that game. It was a different role," Vardell recalls.

That would be how Vardell's first season with the Browns would mostly go: a big part of the offense one week, mostly an afterthought as a lead blocker the next.

In 1992 Vardell ran for 369 yards on 99 carries but was unable to score a touchdown in his first season.

The following year was better, as he crossed the goal line three times, and ended the season with 644 yards for the Browns on the ground.

That would be the peak of his career with the Browns. The following two years he was injured for most of both seasons, playing in a total of ten games.

It was something that hurt Vardell; some Browns fans didn't seem to care that he was trying hard to fight through the injuries that kept him off the field.

"I carried a lot of pain with me over the years after what should have been a career-ending injury and basically missing parts of the '94 and '95 seasons, which all culminated in the Browns' move to Baltimore.

"But these struggles are what shape and prepare people for life. And I think most Browns fans understand that."

Vardell left the Browns organization as the team moved to Baltimore in 1996 and signed a deal with the San Francisco 49ers, moving back to northern California, where his football career had started at Stanford.

He had two different stints with the 49ers, in 1996 and again in 1999, but in between had two memorable seasons with the Detroit Lions.

The first season in Detroit, Vardell was a main factor in helping Hall of Famer Barry Sanders have his all-time best season, one in which he rushed for 2,053 yards and 11 touchdowns.

The following season, Sanders ran for near 1,500 yards, with Vardell again helping out in a big way as the team's fullback, who was solid in short-yardage situations, leading the team with seven rushing touchdowns.

His retirement from the game hasn't seen Vardell slow down whatsoever. Using his college degree in industrial engineering, he co-founded Northgate Capital, a Private Equity Investment Firm that manages $5BB in assets.

He has been active in multiple charitable projects, youth sports, and literacy programs. He was named Cleveland Touchdown Club Alumni of the Year for his donations to Cleveland area charities. He also was the key donor for the Meadows Turkey Bowl, which has donated over $1MM to families in need across the Cleveland area.

He has served on a number of company boards and is currently vice chair of the alumni services committee at the Stanford Alumni Association.

His football career has been over for 17 years, but he still has good feelings about his time in Cleveland and maintains a bond with the fans.

"My relationships with fans were deep and wonderful when I was in Cleveland," Vardell said.

"I felt like we understood each other. We shared the value of work, struggle, dedication, camaraderie, and the team culture.

"I got to see firsthand the generational importance of the Browns to the city and was very active in my communications (via mail and TV) with them. I also spoke at a number of Browns' backers events across the United States.

"In Cleveland, game jerseys are worn year around, before and after games, to work, to parties, over business attire, to weddings.

"And I haven't seen brown and orange on the pages of GQ lately— or ever. These are some serious fans."

CHAPTER 22

ED SUTTER

Linebacker 1993–1995
The Game: December 10, 1994, vs Dallas Cowboys at Texas Stadium
CLEVELAND BROWNS 19—DALLAS COWBOYS 14

THE CLEVELAND BROWNS in the Bill Belichick era was a team built primarily on two things—defense and special teams.

If there was one thing you could count on week in and week out, it was a prepared defense and a lot of hard hitting and emotion on special teams.

One of the key players on Belichick's special teams during his time with the Browns was a linebacker from Northwestern named Ed Sutter.

He came to the team after he was undrafted in 1992, then signed as a free agent with the Minnesota Vikings before eventually landing with the Browns.

"It was a great time," Sutter said of coming to the Browns in 1993. "It was neat to be in a city where the team was a big part of the city. Cleveland rallied around the Browns. It was really neat to be a part of."

Sutter was born and raised in Peoria, Illinois, and started playing football in the sixth grade. In high school at Richwoods, he helped his team to a second-place finish in Class 5A in 1987.

He was a good linebacker but also in high school practiced punting, something he enjoyed as he got ready for college at Northwestern.

Notes on Ed Sutter

Years Played: 1993-1995
Position: Linebacker
Height: 6'3"
Weight: 240
Hometown: Peoria, IL
Current Residence: Peoria, IL
Occupation: Financial Adviser with Morgan Stanley
Accomplishments: Was a part in helping his Richwoods High School football team to a second-place finish in Class 5A in 1987. He was an all-star as well as second-team prep All-American as a senior when Richwoods fell to Joliet Catholic in the 5A title game by a score of 14–13. He moved on to Northwestern and ended his college career as its fourth-leading career tackler with 429 total tackles. He also was the Wildcats' MVP in both 1990 and 1992. He led the league in tackles with 161 in 1990. Played for six seasons in the NFL, mostly as a standout special teams player. He started with the Browns for three seasons, played one year with the Ravens in Baltimore, and then with the Atlanta Falcons. Inducted to the Greater Peoria Sports Hall of Fame in 2003. Lives in Peoria with his wife and five kids and is a successful Financial Adviser with Morgan Stanley.
Nickname: None

Linebacker Ed Sutter was also a special teams standout with the Browns. (Photo courtesy of Ed Sutter)

"I thought about just punting at the pro level, and to me I thought I had I chance to play linebacker, which I obviously did, but punting was an option, as well; but I didn't pursue it because I enjoyed playing linebacker," Sutter said.

The success he found at Richwoods he didn't match at Northwestern in terms of winning, because the Wildcats won just seven games, losing 36 and tying one in his time at the school.

"In high school I had success, then I went on to college at Northwestern, where obviously we didn't win much. That was the pre-Gary Barnett era where we struggled to win, but still obviously I got a lot of attention there," Sutter recalls.

In college Sutter found individual success. He was a two-time All-Big Ten linebacker and led the league in tackles in 1990 with 161.

In 1990 and 1992, he was also the team MVP and is the Wildcats' fourth all-time career tackler with 429.

He came to the Browns in the midst of the Bill Belichick regime. By then the coach had already started to establish himself and the way he wanted things done, and was doing it his way.

"He was pretty reserved. He was younger," Sutter said of Belichick.

"I would say he was a little more laid back, certainly, compared to college coaches. He kind of let guys do what they wanted to do, and that was I think one of the better things about him. He studied and did all the research, and I think some players he didn't expect to know a whole lot.

"So he would put players in positions, make things simple for them and let them play, and I think that was one of the great things about him. It seemed like he did the research and the studying for a lot of these guys.

"He would have some guys who were coaches on the field. But more than half the guys, he would line up good athletes and let them play and put them in the right positions. That's probably why he's so successful. Nobody studies and prepares teams like he does."

In Sutter's first season with the Browns in 1993, the team started the season 5–2, but then after Belichick made a tough decision to release beloved quarterback Bernie Kosar, it sent the team in a tailspin, and they won just two games the rest of the season.

Things, though, took quite a turn for the team in 1994, Belichick's best in his tenure with the Browns.

The Browns' defense played as well as about any in the NFL, and their special teams were also good at both returning and covering kicks that season, something Sutter had plenty to do with.

The team was 9–3 and neck and neck with the rival Pittsburgh Steelers for control of the AFC Central, but then were upset at home by the New York Giants, 16–13, on December 4th to fall to 9–4.

Up next was a critical game that was not going to be easy, a game in Dallas at Texas Stadium against the defending Super Bowl Champion Dallas Cowboys.

A game that Sutter will never forget.

The Game

I think the time that was most memorable in my time with the Browns was the game in Dallas in 1994.

That game was kind of what put us over the top, and we're going to the playoffs.

We beat a solid team, and I think that was the game where we realized we were there, and I think the city did, as well.

I think that was probably one of the bigger ones. Everything leading up to that was big, but that one kind of put us over the hump, and we realized we were going to the playoffs and had a real shot to do well.

We were big underdogs, but going in we had a lot of confidence. I think the team in general had a lot of confidence.

We prepared really well. The guys really rallied around what we were doing and believed.

I think when I was there it seemed like the offense took a lot of heat and they were not able to generate much, but I think once Bill kind of moved on and was able to figure that out we really took off, because the defense had you just focused on defense and special teams. The teams he coached were some of the best ever, probably.

I don't know if he was the first, but maybe because I played special teams I noticed that, boy, his focus on special teams was huge.

It was just a huge part of his game. We had the best special teams in the league, I think, every year I was there. If not the best, then close to it. And you know, our kickoff teams nobody got past the 20–25 yard line most times.

Our coverage units and return teams, especially when you throw Eric Metcalf back there, and some of our schemes as far as breaking him free, were huge.

So special teams were a huge part of it. Defense was a huge part. Offense was the one area, obviously, I wasn't involved in it, but was the one area that struggled, and once Bill kind of figured that out, that's what kind of set him free.

Belichick was my first pro coach so I didn't really know anything different. But after I left I looked back and realized, "Wow. We were so prepared."

We did everything kind of over the top as far as practice, preparation, detail. Everything was on so much of a higher level than all the other teams I was on, and all the other coaches that I played for.

Another thing about him is that he was very involved in the special teams. He would sit in on the meetings a lot of times.

He was involved in everything. He would watch guys do bag drills. On film. Some of the stuff he would do it was like, "You've got to be kidding me."

Some of the stuff he would focus on was not even on other coaches' radars. But you know what, he was good to play for, too. He was loyal to his players, and mainly the guys who really worked hard, he was super loyal to. He would do almost anything for you.

I think guys in New England see that, and when a coach is that loyal to you, you really want to do well for them.

There were a couple of players that probably didn't see that, and if you didn't work hard for him he wasn't going to go to bat for you, but if you worked really hard for him he'd do anything for you.

All the preparation paid off that day in Dallas; we had a 16–7 lead, and they closed it to 16–14 when Matt Stover hit a field goal to get us up, 19–14.

They got the ball back one last time, and I was on special teams so I wasn't on defense for that final drive, but I was on the sidelines and it was really exciting.

At any point there could have been a big break for a touchdown and it was kind of "bend, but don't break" and we kind of held firm when it really counted.

Guys made big plays all year. We had some really good players out there and it was exciting, and once we won it was a real sense of accomplishment.

The last play Eric Turner made a saving tackle on their tight end, Jay Novacek, at the goal line, and at the time we kind of didn't know for sure, but with the signal and everything never saw the touchdown sign, so it was fantastic.

It was just a great night and great rest of the season, really. We had momentum going into it and never really lost it. Things just continued to go our way.

The Aftermath

The huge win in Dallas was followed by a tough 17–7 loss to the Steelers in Pittsburgh, in a game that gave the Steelers the division as well as home field in the AFC for the 1994 playoffs.

The Browns won their final regular season game that season, a 35–9 victory over the Seattle Seahawks, which set up a home wild-card game on New Year's Day against the New England Patriots.

Belichick and his team beat Bill Parcells and New England, 20–13, which set up a third showdown with the Steelers, a divisional playoff game in which the Browns were beaten badly, 29–9.

"We took care of business at home against New England. We felt like we had the confidence that they were not at our level, and it didn't seem like we struggled too much with New England," Sutter said.

"Pittsburgh had our number all year, and it was our third game against them. They had that off-tackle play that would get them rolling downhill, and it gave us fits. We just couldn't find a way to beat them."

It appeared that 1994 was a stepping stone for the Browns, and many had them picked to make an even bigger impact in 1995.

No one expected the complete demise of the franchise as team owner Art Modell announced in November that the club would move to Baltimore starting in 1996, taking the team away from its beloved fan base in Cleveland.

"Going into the '95 season we had a lot of momentum," Sutter said. "We had gotten to the playoffs in '94 and had a pretty good year there. A really good year, actually. There was a lot of expectation going into the '95 season.

"Unfortunately, it didn't really pan out, and a lot of things happened, but it was neat to be a part of the franchise."

Sutter played one season with the new former Browns franchise in Baltimore and then moved on to the Atlanta Falcons, where he played the 1997 season before his football career concluded, sooner than he may have wanted it to.

"My last year in Atlanta I was probably the best player that I had ever been," Sutter said. "I pulled a hamstring in Atlanta during training camp, and that kind of slowed me down all year.

"I tried to fight through it and play through it, but I kind of kept re-injuring it. Before that, things were going great. In pro football I kind of knew that if you're special teams or a regular position as you get older, you don't have a lot of chances. So I had bounced around. I went from Baltimore, signed with Cincinnati, they released me, and I got picked up by Atlanta, so I kind of felt like you know, once you've bounced around a little bit if things don't go right you have to have a little luck. And luck is staying healthy, so unfortunately I had a little injury at the wrong time."

The former linebacker took to another field after he left the game: he became a financial adviser with Morgan Stanley in Peoria, Illinois, where he lives today with his wife and five kids.

"We got three girls and two boys. It'll be a while before they play football," Sutter laughed.

"Maybe they'll eventually play. I coach everything I can. I want to be involved with them as much as possible.

"I figure I'm going to the games, I'm going to go and watch them, so I might as well help them out. I know as much about most of these sports as anybody else, so why not?"

CHAPTER 23

JOE DELAMIELLEURE

Guard 1980–1984
The Game: January 4, 1981, vs Oakland Raiders at Cleveland Stadium
OAKLAND RAIDERS 14—CLEVELAND BROWNS 12

TWO WORDS WOULD best describe Pro Football Hall of Fame offensive guard Joe DeLamielleure: durable and dependable.

DeLamielleure played in an amazing 185 consecutive games during his 13 playing seasons with the Buffalo Bills and the Cleveland Browns, after having been selected as a first-round pick by the Bills (26th overall) in the 1973 NFL Draft.

Right from the start he was a leader on an offensive line that became a part of NFL history. A key member of the famous "Electric Company," DeLamielleure helped fellow Hall of Famer O.J. Simpson reach a mark in 1973 that no back had ever achieved, rushing for over 2,000 yards in just 14 regular season games.

Born in Detroit, Michigan, on March 15, 1961, DeLamielleure was the ninth of ten children in a huge family, and played his high school ball at St.Clement High School in Center Line, before attending college close to home at Michigan State.

There it became apparent just how good the player eventually known as "Joe D" was. He had been named a three-time All-Big Ten selection and Sporting News All-American by the time he went into the NFL Draft in 1973.

Notes on Joe DeLamielleure

Years Played: 1980–1984
Position: Offensive Guard
Height: 6'3"
Weight: 254
Hometown: Detroit, Michigan
Current Residence: Charlotte, NC
Occupation: Operates a fitness equipment firm
Accomplishments: Part of the famous Buffalo Bills offensive line called "The Electric Company" that helped Hall of Fame RB O.J. Simpson, in 1973, become the first player ever to rush for over 2,000 yards in a season. Was drafted by the Bills in the first round of the 1973 NFL Draft and played seven seasons there before being traded to Cleveland before the 1980 season. Become the first player ever to block for a 2,000-yard rusher (Simpson) and a 4,000-yard passer (Cleveland's Brian Sipe), as well as for two NFL MVPs in Simpson and Sipe. Played every game in his five seasons with the Browns. Was a six-time Pro Bowl selection, as well as a six-time first-team All-Pro selection. Earned the Forrest Gregg Award as, the NFL Offensive Lineman of the Year in 1977. Went head-to-head against Pittsburgh Steelers Hall of Fame DE "Mean" Joe Greene eight times in his career, and Greene put up just 15 solo tackles and one sack in those eight games. Made a comeback in 1992 playing with the Charlotte Rage in the AFL.
Nickname: Joe D

The Bills took DeLamielleure, and he immediately paid dividends as the centerpiece of a line that helped Simpson make history.

He, along with Reggie McKenzie, Pau Seymour, Dave Foley, and Mike Montler, formed as dominant an offensive line as the NFL had ever seen.

The Bills had three winning seasons with the line intact, including a 32–14 playoff loss at Pittsburgh in the 1974 season against the eventual Super Bowl Champion Steelers.

DeLamielleure also helped Simpson rush for a then-single game record 273 yards on Thanksgiving Day, November 25, 1976, in a Bills' 27–14 loss at Detroit against the Lions.

On September 1, 1980, the Browns made a move with the Bills that would land them DeLamielleure, who just a month before had been named to the 1970s All-Decade team.

The Browns gave up a second-round draft choice in 1981 and their third-rounder in 1982, a steal for a player the caliber of DeLamielleure. Little did the guard know that he was entering a Browns team in 1980 that he has since called "the best he's ever played on."

In 1979 the Browns were 9–7, but poised for bigger and better things for 1980, and adding DeLamielleure six days before the season was a key piece to the puzzle.

The team gave Cleveland fans a level of excitement on the football field they had not seen in many years. The club was affectionately known as "The Kardiac Kids," because of their last-second wins and comebacks.

The team won its first division title in nine seasons, winning the AFC Central in a tiebreaker over the Houston Oilers and making the postseason for the first time since 1972.

In what was to follow for the Browns' first playoff game in January 1981 was a game that would go down in Cleveland sports history as one of the more painful memories, and a game that DeLamielleure would talk about as the most memorable in his career.

One play—"Red Right 88"—still lives on as one of the great heartaches in Browns history.

On a day that saw the temperature at kickoff register a -16 with the wind chill, the Browns and Raiders played one of the coldest games in NFL history.

To make matters worse, the grass field at old Cleveland Stadium was nowhere near as well maintained as the fields of today's NFL, and with the wind and temperatures, the game was played as more of a matter of survival than one of skill.

"The field was horrible; I played on high school fields in Detroit where six teams play on it over a weekend and they were not as bad," DeLamielleure recalled about the field that afternoon in Cleveland.

"Jayne Field in Detroit, you had games Friday afternoon and Friday night, two games on Saturday, and a game on Sunday. That was a better field than the one at Cleveland Stadium."

The result was a Browns 14–12 loss to the Raiders, who three weeks later beat the Philadelphia Eagles in Super Bowl XV in New Orleans.

The Game

Everybody knows the game, "Red Right 88." Everybody knew, I knew, it was going to be a tough game, and playing in Buffalo for eight years I was used to playing in cold weather.

When you played in Buffalo and it was cold, at least you were playing on Astroturf.

Playing in Cleveland it was natural grass, and what they did was, when we went out on the field I knew it was going to be frozen, but there were tractor tire marks all over the field where they pulled the tarp off.

Even the tracks froze over, and the field was totally frozen. So the field made it the worst conditions I had ever played in, or ever saw in a game.

I knew there would be no advantage. I remember people saying, "Hey, the Raiders won't be used to the weather," but I knew that it would all come down to luck, and it did.

The conditions took away a lot, if not all, of the skill.

We had a much better team than Oakland, that's what I thought. We just didn't have any luck; we missed two extra points, and that was the game.

Missing those two extra points took all the confidence from (Browns coach) Sam Rutigliano trying to kick a field goal, so that's what turned that game around.

We should have won that game; we should have kicked that field goal, and we should have won, 15–14, in the end.

We could run the ball; we got it at our 15-yard line and got it all the way down to the Raiders' 13-yard line on that final drive when the game basically ended.

The game was basically Mike and Greg Pruitt running the ball.

There was no advantage for anybody, so we knew it was going to come down to a lucky break. The lucky break is that we missed two extra points, that was the lucky break.

I always look back at that game and say that it was my best chance to get to the Super Bowl.

There was a time in 1974 we played the Steelers in the playoffs when I was with the Bills, and we were the victim of a bad call. But that was a bad call, and a bad call is just that—a bad call, that's the way it goes.

A field where you know you are the better team, and the field was just so bad, nothing mattered. You just couldn't move.

I can't believe it; the Vikings played the Seahawks in the playoffs in Minnesota this past season, and it was almost exactly the same thing, except they attempted the field goal and he missed it.

I do think the Seahawks in that game were the much better team, but the difference is they won, and back in that game against Oakland we didn't.

That last drive, we were making plays going downfield, and I remember sitting there thinking we would just kick the field goal and win it, and it would be over.

That's how we did it the whole year, and we all thought that's how it was going to finish. Sure enough, it went to the last seconds.

I thought instead of passing we would just run it to the center hash and kick a field goal. I didn't think we would throw it, and I'm not saying that was the wrong call or not, that's just how I felt.

I remember the "Red Right 88" play very well; the ball actually zoomed right by my fat head when Brian Sipe threw it. I wish I would have hit it.

I remember seeing Mike Davis (the Raiders' safety) come up with it in front of Ozzie Newsome in the end zone.

I actually talked to Mike once and told him I don't like him. I said, "I don't know you, but I don't like you, either."

The Raiders ended up playing Philadelphia in the Super Bowl, and Philadelphia could have never played with us, I don't think so anyway.

We had better players all the way around. Sipe was better than (Raiders QB Jim) Plunkett that year, we had better receivers, our defense was pretty darn good. All the way around, I thought we had a better team than Oakland.

Usually you don't feel that way; in the NFL just about every game is a toss-up, but that game I really felt we were a better team, we had better players.

The problem was I just knew that, with conditions like that, skill doesn't have a lot to do with it. I knew it was going to come down to a break, something lucky was going to happen of some sort, a fumble, an interception, a dropped kick.

The Aftermath

The heartache of losing the "Red Right 88" game to the Raiders was as tough as any loss in the history of the Browns organization.

The team felt it would use the disappointment of the 1980 season as a stepping stone into 1981, but it was not meant to be. Its record in '81 was just 5–11.

After a season in 1980 of close wins, in 1981 it was just the opposite. The Browns played in eight games that were decided by six points or less, and five were decided by three points or less.

While Sipe was again very good in 1981, it didn't translate into wins, and it seemed that all the magic the team had the season before was simply gone.

DeLamielleure was his usual fantastic self on the field, playing at a high level for the next four seasons until he retired from the NFL.

He remains to this day very outspoken about the conditions of Cleveland Stadium, as well as the overall conditions NFL players played in during the era in which he played.

"Anytime anyone said or was upset that (Browns owner Art) Modell was moving the team, I would say to myself, 'Yeah, he's moving the team because they won't fix the stadium.'

"The locker rooms stunk, too. The visiting locker room you only had three working showers. Guys who play nowadays, they have no idea what the former guys went through. They really don't; they would never play in those conditions," DeLamielleure said.

"Philadelphia, the old Vet where the Eagles played, that place sucked, they had gaps in the turf, Brian Billick of the Ravens took his team off the field in a preseason game.

"We played all the time on that field.

"When I got traded to Cleveland, we were in the old AFC Central with Pittsburgh, Houston, and Cincinnati. It's no wonder those teams had the best hitters in baseball, they were all playing on concrete."

In 2003, DeLamielleure received the highest honor a player could ever get: he was selected for induction into the Pro Football Hall of Fame.

The honor came despite his outspoken nature about the way the game is played today, as well as never being afraid to speak up about how he felt players of the past were not treated fairly.

"I'm glad I played football when I did. I liked the way the game was then. The people, though, that made the game what it is today are not being taken care of," DeLamielleure said.

"I think that is criminal. The pre-1993 guys, we have subpar pensions and no health care, that's sick. They are not going to change it, they don't care.

"When the commissioner (Roger Goodell) makes $44 million dollars, it's hard for him to relate to somebody who doesn't have health care.

"I like the game, and I like some of the kids who play it now, but It's pretty hard to swallow, to tell you the truth."

DeLamielleure has an interesting opinion about the Browns team he once played on, going so far as believing the Browns franchise he played on for five seasons now plays in another city.

"Cleveland right now, that's not the Cleveland Browns, that's not the same team. The management is totally different. The real Browns are in Baltimore.

"It's never been the same, and it's just too bad. I was born in Detroit, drafted by Buffalo, traded to Cleveland. Between the three of them, not one Super Bowl win.

"That's a long time, no Super Bowls. When I was a kid, the Lions and Browns were playing for NFL championships."

ACKNOWLEDGEMENTS

FIRST AND FOREMOST, I dedicate this book to my Lord and Savior, Jesus Christ, for without him none of this would be possible. To my loving wife, Shanna, who has always been a great source of encouragement and has always stood by me through the wild ride that has been this book, as well as through my career.

To my loving family, my mom and dad for their loving support, brothers John, Russell, and Michael, sisters-in-law Mary Ann, Terri, and Kim, and eight nieces and nephews for their love through the years. To my wonderful in-laws for their support and understanding.

To my friends for their help in this project: Matt Medley, Vince McKee, Tracie Potts, Lindsey Foltin, Kenny Roda, Sue Ann Roback, Kevin Byrne; Mark Quinn; and friends Charles Spooner, Melanie Cramer, Josh Thompson, Dave Hummel, T.J. Zuppe, Tim Alcorn, Greg Buk, Ed Emrich, Steve Emrich, Karl Jeske, Ryan Kaczmarski, Mike Coutee, Adrienne Goehler, Brandon Urasek, Jim Koney, Dan McVey, Joe Simonetta, Kate Mueller; Sujeet Patel, John Sefcik, Matt Sefcik, and the best karate teacher ever in Mark Miller; and all my other friends, as well as students and staff at the Ohio Media School.

And finally, to my church family at Cleveland Baptist Church for always keeping my feet on the ground. Pastor Kevin Folger, Pete Folger, and Sandra Folger, Jack Beaver, Daniel Wu, Rich Gibson, Ron Van Kirk, Kevin Hoffman, Ryan Zapsic, Doug Schweitzer, Jeremy Cron, Todd and Julia Lapp, Tim Kardamis, Tim Hanrahan, Bill Yeager, Kevin Grimm, Al Varwig, and all the rest. Thank you for all your support.

To Browns Backers and Browns Fans everywhere.